Desalination and Water Security

T0309242

Desalination is to the water industry what renewables are to the electricity sector. However, unlike renewables, the former is being deployed in a quiet revolution away from public glare.

This book provides a holistic view of desalination, highlighting the important role this technology can play in providing safe access to water across the globe. It describes the context for this technology to flourish in the coming decades. It discusses the pressures on freshwater resources and the key role the desalination industry plays as it moves from a good-to-have provider today to a must-have mainstream water solution in the future. The book explores the vital elements of the desalination industry, including the winning technologies and how further technological developments will reduce costs and increase deployment into new areas. It also addresses the energy used and the key environmental issues of carbon dioxide emissions and brine waste production. Using a series of country case studies, the book illustrates how desalination can supplement natural water resources in different environments and for different purposes, and how it is supporting domestic and economic activity. Providing a forward-thinking assessment, the book considers developments over the next 30 years as climate change impacts become even more apparent.

This book will be of great interest to those working to alleviate water scarcity and improve water security. It will also be of interest to those in water resource management, water policy and regulation, water science, and environmental engineering.

Chris Anastasi is an industry professional, academic, consultant, and author. He is an expert on energy, climate change, and other environmental issues related to sustainable development and in scenario analysis. He has worked for major international companies and acted as an advisor to national and international institutions. He was previously a Senior Lecturer at the University of York in the UK and acted as a Visiting-Professor at the University of Maastricht in the Netherlands. He is the author of two books, *Strategic Stakeholder Engagement* (Routledge, 2018) and *Who Needs Nuclear Power* (Routledge, 2021).

Earthscan Studies in Water Resource Management

Water Management and Violent Conflict in East Africa
Scarcity and Security in Kenya and Uganda
Julia Renner-Mugono

Water Scarcity and Conflict in African River Basins
The Hydropolitical Landscape
Mahlakeng Khosi Mahlakeng

River Basins and International Relations
Cooperation, Conflict and Sub-Regional Approaches
Edited by Christian Ploberger

New Perspectives on Transboundary Water Governance
Interdisciplinary Approaches and Global Case Studies
Edited by Luis Paulo Batista da Silva, Wagner Costa Ribeiro, and Isabela Battistello Espíndola

The Role of Law in Transboundary River Basin Disputes
Cooperation and Peaceful Settlement
Chukwuebuka Edum

Desalination and Water Security
Chris Anastasi

Flood Risk and Community Resilience
An Interdisciplinary Approach
Lindsey Jo McEwen

For more information about this series, please visit: www.routledge.com/books/series/ECWRM/

Desalination and Water Security

Chris Anastasi

LONDON AND NEW YORK

Designed cover image: © Shutterstock

First published 2024
by Routledge
4 Park Square, Milton Park, Abingdon, Oxon OX14 4RN

and by Routledge
605 Third Avenue, New York, NY 10158

Routledge is an imprint of the Taylor & Francis Group, an informa business

British Library Cataloguing-in-Publication Data
A catalogue record for this book is available from the British Library

ISBN: 978-1-032-36869-6 (hbk)
ISBN: 978-1-032-36867-2 (pbk)
ISBN: 978-1-003-33422-4 (ebk)

DOI: 10.4324/9781003334224

Typeset in Times New Roman
by KnowledgeWorks Global Ltd.

For those who have helped me on my way,
in particular Professors Bill Price, Ian Smith,
and David Waddington, and Roger Rainbow,
Robert Armour, Bill Coley, and Steve Riley.

Contents

Figures

Tables

Foreword

With global shifting weather patterns, rising temperatures, a growing population, and expanding global industrial developments, the demand for reliable, clean, and potable water has reached unprecedented levels.

Approximately 71% of the Earth's surface is covered by water, of which 97.4% is saltwater. Except for surface water and some groundwater, most of the freshwater is not readily accessible for human use. In dry areas, over-extraction of the groundwater has often resulted in land subsidence.

The current climate crisis has thrust the issue of water scarcity to the forefront and has demanded innovative solutions to tackle such a pressing global challenge. Desalination technologies in general, and particularly membrane-based desalination technologies with their ability to convert abundant saltwater into freshwater, could provide a great opportunity for a more sustainable future.

In the last two decades, with advancements in technology and engineering, desalination has evolved from a niche concept to a viable and scalable method of producing pure water. It has been playing a vital role in dry regions such as the Middle East and North Africa region, have prolonged droughts and unreliable rainfall. In addition, desalination technology has provided increased resilience of water supply in coastal regions, which are often densely populated and prone to water stress. In the United States, California and Texas are prime examples of such applications. In those regions, desalinated water is also used for aquifer recharge.

Another application of the membrane-based desalination technology at smaller scales is during disastrous events where the availability of freshwater supply is critical. Containerised desalination plants have been utilised where access to seawater is readily available.

While desalination technology presents a promising solution, it is not without its challenges. Energy consumption, environmental impacts, and cost-effectiveness are among the key considerations that must be addressed to ensure the long-term viability and sustainability of desalination projects.

Overall, desalination technology has emerged as a game-changer in the pursuit of water security in our rapidly changing climate. This technology has great potential to improve water scarcity and promote sustainable development.

Dr Abraham Negaresh, Thames Gateway Desalination Plant,
Thames Water Utilities, UK

It is easy to think when you live in the UK that you live in a water-abundant society. In fact, our popular culture is littered with 'the rain,' whether that be our recollections of wet Wimbledon tournaments or my own memories of wet summer holidays with my family. The reality is different, however, and climate change has had a significant impact on rainfall within London and South-East England. This region receives roughly the same amount of rainfall as Jerusalem every year, and with predictions that the temperature will continue to rise in the forthcoming years, suppliers, legislators, and the public need to consider their relationship with both the production and consumption of our most precious resource.

Thames Water opened the Thames Gateway (previously Beckton) desalination plant in 2010 with a design capacity of around 150 million litres of water a day (able to service the needs of about 400,000 households). It was the first of its kind in the UK and more commonly seen in countries with higher water stress than the UK. It was built because of two major drivers that were emerging at the time. Firstly, ongoing climate change would increase water stress, and secondly, the population of London would increase by around 700,000 people by 2021. Both assumptions have turned out to be true, with the actual population of the London area increasing by about a million people over the same period.

The plant does not exist to provide a daily water supply as the economics of producing water via the Reverse Osmosis technology versus normal water production do not really make sense – particularly in a high energy cost environment - but it is designed to provide an important role as a short-to-medium-term solution in periods of high-water stress and exists largely in that contingency capacity.

As we think about water resilience in the southeast of England over the coming years, we have an impetus across the water sector to reduce waste of water both within the supply networks but also within consumers' homes. Several schemes to address water shortages are currently being proposed across the southeast, although none will replicate the desalination plant in place now. Whilst there are new sites being proposed in the southwest of England, these will take several years to come online, so for the UK mainland at least, the Thames Gateway desalination plant remains one of its kind.

This book is timely, providing a holistic view of the industry at an important time in its development. It discusses the changing context for the desalination industry as the impacts of climate change become even more apparent and introduces the technologies involved and their implications for energy and the environment. The book also illustrates the use of desalination across the world through a series of country case studies. It also explores its potential role in the middle of this century to better understand whether the industry can provide the level of water security needed in a challenging global environment.

David Wylie, Director of Commercial and Procurement,
Thames Water Utilities, UK

Preface

To quote my great-grandfather, *life is sweet*. This is made possible by the ready availability of freshwater, which is critical to the well-being of people and the environment they inhabit. Rising populations, economic development, and the depletion of natural reservoirs have made water a major issue in many regions of the world. Changing weather patterns, brought about by man-made perturbations to the natural environment, will make matters worse. Government and industry around the world will have to address water shortages in their countries, in some cases severe and for extended periods.

On the book content

Climate change is a key issue for the world today. The introduction to this book in Chapter 1 discusses the drivers for this phenomenon, the emission of carbon dioxide and other greenhouse gases, and the associated rise in global temperatures. The response by decision-makers has been less than is needed, and the indications are that the world will fail to meet targets agreed for 2050. There are major implications for renewable freshwater resources and water scarcity; the extent of the problem and potential solutions are explored in Chapter 2.

Technology, in the form of desalination, can help alleviate the problem. In many ways, this technology is to the water industry what renewables are to the electricity sector, the difference being that desalination is being deployed in a quiet revolution away from the public glare. The aim of this book is to take a holistic view of the desalination industry, highlighting its benefits and its limitations. It will describe the changing context for the technology in the coming decades as it moves from a 'good-to-have' contributor to the freshwater provision to a 'must-have', mainstream water solution, particularly for the domestic sector. The conditions for this transformation will be discussed, and the potential scale of its contribution to water supply and the associated implications for energy, and the environment will be assessed over the period to 2050.

As indicated above, the key drivers for increasing pressure on freshwater supplies in many parts of the world are discussed in Chapter 2 with a particular focus on the role of population growth, economic development, and climate change. The latter increases the pressure on supplies in some regions today and will do so increasingly over the next thirty years, and the interplay between climate change, energy and the provision of freshwater supplies will be explored.

The status of the industry is established in Chapter 3, including the number and regional distribution of the plants commissioned, the types of technologies deployed, and the production capacity. Key aspects of the desalination industry, including the quality of water delivered, the economics of production and the price of water, and the 'winning' technologies, are discussed. Technological development and 'learning', both of which reduce costs and make deployment into new jurisdictions easier, are also explored. Energy and the environment are important considerations for the industry, and the way in which both of these issues determine the nature of the technologies adopted and the scale of deployment is discussed in Chapter 4. The role of the key stakeholders in encouraging or opposing the deployment of this critical water infrastructure is also an important consideration.

A series of country case studies are presented in Chapter 5 that serve to illustrate the remarkable geographical reach of the industry. They also cover key aspects of each country, including the renewable freshwater and groundwater resources, the desalination technology adopted, the nature of the feedwater for the process, how the water produced is used, and the availability or otherwise of indigenous energy supplies. The increasingly important role of desalination in supplementing natural water resources in different regions is highlighted, and the country case studies presented illustrate how desalination is playing an important role in water provision for domestic consumption and economic activity.

It is important to assess how the industry will evolve in the crucial period to 2050. Looking ahead, then, converging developments that could lead to rapid growth in the deployment of this technology are highlighted. They include trends in society, the political arena, economic activity, technical progress, and their interaction. Such converging developments are captured in several scenario analyses carried out by internationally renowned institutions, and it is possible to draw on them to create simple analytical descriptions of the future. Potential scenarios for the deployment of desalination technology in the period to the middle of this century are developed in Chapter 6 and provide some insights into the overall production capacity, the number of plants needed to deliver it, and the implications for energy consumption and the environment.

Having taken a holistic view of desalination, Chapter 7 provides some reflections on the importance of this technology as a source of pure water alongside the other options. It highlights the key role that desalination will play in the future, particularly in the provision of drinking water in some countries. It is a global industry, set to grow significantly over the next two or three decades, and as such, there will continue to be new entrants into the supply chain, bringing new innovations and approaches.

On the information and data used in the book

The water and energy industries are intimately linked with one another. There are, however, important differences in the quality of the data and information available. The energy industry has been international in nature almost from its beginning in the early twentieth century, with governments taking a keen interest in the sector and major companies emerging to service the needs of markets around the world. The climate change issue has also shone a spotlight on energy and the need for accurate data at the national, regional, and global level, and this has been forthcoming.

The water industry, on the other hand, is made up of national markets, and, except for rivers, there is little transport of this resource across national borders. The lack of an international market for water removes an important driver for comprehensive, harmonised, and reliable data sets over an extended period. The water scarcity issue, with climate change an important contributor, is driving interest in data and information about national water resources, including desalination.

The analyses presented in this book draw on the data published by institutions such as the World Bank and the United Nations and some excellent published papers in learned journals. The sources do not necessarily cover the same periods or focus on the same issues, and it is sometimes difficult to reconcile the data and information presented across publications. Nonetheless, the key observations derived from the various data sets are broadly consistent and can provide a picture of the evolution of, for example, the available renewable freshwater resources, water scarcity, and the role of desalination in meeting the needs of a burgeoning global population.

Chris Anastasi, November 2023

Acknowledgements

I would like to thank Hannah Ferguson and Katie Stokes at Routledge, who saw merit in the subject matter and helped steer me through its publication. I am very grateful for their advice, support, and patience, which made writing the book easier and enjoyable.

My interest in desalination started in the 1990s, when I was working on scenario development with the fabled Shell Group Planning Team. I helped developed Shell's first long-term energy scenarios, which covered the period 1860–2060 and it was clear then that water scarcity would be an increasingly challenging issue and that desalination was an important emerging technology. It is appropriate, then, that I thank Roger Rainbow for giving me the opportunity to work on such an interesting scenario project.

I was fortunate to visit two operational plants during my research: the Dhekelia Desalination Plant in Cyprus, and the Gateway (formerly Beckton) Desalination Plant in England. These were very helpful site visits, and I would like to thank Demetris Petrou for allowing me to visit the Dhekelia site and Vasiliki Daniel for showing me the plant and David Wylie and Abraham Nagaresh of Thames Water for hosting my visit to Gateway.

I would also like to thank Tony Marinaro and Charlie Morley, Tony for many interesting discussions on the topic of water over the last couple of years, and Charlie for turning my charts into excellent figures in the book.

Finally, I would like to thank my family for their support throughout the writing of this book. I would particularly like to thank my brother Andy, who gave me use of his summer house for extended periods to progress the book and, together with my sister Helen, made sure that I was well fed during my stays in Cyprus.

1 Introduction

Climate change is the defining issue for the 21st century with major implications for freshwater supplies in many regions across the world.

1.1 A challenging world

The world faces many challenges this century. The inexorable rise in population, the drive for economic development, the unsustainable consumption of the earth's resources, and perhaps the most challenging of all, the unravelling of climate change. These converging developments will make for a very uncomfortable world for billions of people. There is hope and expectation that innovation, new technologies, greater resource efficiency, and changing behaviour will help address these challenges as they have in the past. Major investment in new, improved infrastructure in energy, water, transport, and communications *could* facilitate the step-change needed in the period to 2050, but the evidence that this could occur is not promising.

Climate change is the defining issue of the 21st century. Signals indicating a potential change in our climate in the form of increasing atmospheric concentrations of greenhouse gases have been with us for decades. It has long been understood that carbon dioxide (CO_2) and water are greenhouse agents, that is, they are transparent to radiation from the sun and absorb the radiation emitted by the earth; they help maintain the temperature of the atmosphere, and the earth's surface in contact with it, at habitable levels. The physics is clear: increasing the concentration of these and other greenhouse agents increases the absorptive capacity of the atmosphere; this raises the global temperature and changes the climate.

There is, then, a question as to whether it is possible, even at this late stage, to lessen the impacts of this phenomenon and if not, how best to ensure basic needs such as the provision of freshwater for a growing global population are met.

DOI: 10.4324/9781003334224-1

1.2   Carbon dioxide emissions

The scientific evidence for climate change and the impacts on the environment, both global and local, has become increasingly apparent. Human activity leads to increased emissions of carbon dioxide (CO_2), methane (CH_4), nitrous oxide (N_2O), and sulphur hexafluoride (SF_6) gases. Although there are some removal processes for CO_2 and CH_4, the concentrations of all these gases in the atmosphere have risen markedly in the past 50 years or so; their ability to trap the earth's radiation in a 'greenhouse effect' has led to an increase in global temperatures and changing climate patterns.

There are estimates of the cumulative emission of CO_2 into the atmosphere since the start of the industrial revolution and this shows that the United States is by far the largest contributor at around 420 billion tonnes over the period 1750–2020. The next two major contributors are the EU's 27 countries combined and China, emitting an estimated 290 and 230 billion tonnes, respectively. The United Kingdom, the country that led the industrial revolution, has emitted about 80 billion tonnes total during this period.

Carbon dioxide emissions over the period 1965–2020 and those in 2020 are also important metrics. The ten largest CO_2 emitters over the period 1965–2020, cumulatively, were the USA, China, Russia, Japan, Germany, India, the United Kingdom, Canada, France, and Italy. The world's ten largest CO_2 emitters in 2020 were China, the USA, India, Russia, Japan, Iran, Germany, South Korea, Saudi Arabia, and Indonesia; together, these countries emitted 69% of the world's total CO_2 emissions; many of the countries listed are present in both metrics. It is incumbent, then, on these countries to step up their greenhouse gas emission reduction efforts since they have gained most from the use of fossil fuels over the past 50 years.

To these countries must be added Brazil because of its pivotal role in deforestation over the past few decades, an activity that releases large quantities of CO_2 stored as biomass. This activity also paves the way for other economic activity, such as cattle farming, and this results in further greenhouse gas emissions. Although Brazil is the custodian of this valuable forest resource, it is important the developed and richer nations provide financial and other support to maintain it for the world.

1.3   Atmospheric concentrations of greenhouse gases

The concentration of CO_2 in the atmosphere in the pre-industrial period of the 18th century was just 280 parts per million (ppm) and had remained at about this level for the last million years or so. Since then, it has risen significantly, driven by the combustion of fossil fuels, first by coal, which underpinned the industrial revolution, and then by oil, which facilitated the emergence of mass transport systems on land, air, and sea; most recently, gas has been the preferred fuel for domestic heating and power generation. Deforestation in many

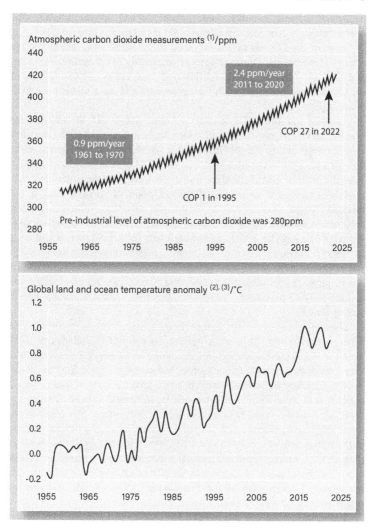

Figure 1.1 Rise in atmospheric carbon dioxide and global temperatures

Sources: (1), Data from the Global Monitoring Laboratory, Earth System Research Laboratories, NOAA; (2), Global land and ocean temperature anomalies 1880–2022, Erick Burgueño Salas, Statista, April 2023.

Note: (3), Temperature anomalies represent the difference from an average or baseline temperature, in this case the 20th century average. ppm, parts per million; COP, Conference of the Parties.

parts of the world also released large quantities of CO_2 into the atmosphere as countries sought economic development for their growing populations.

Some of the CO_2 emitted is absorbed by the earth's vegetation and the oceans. However, the estimated absorptive capacity of the earth's biosystem and oceans appears to have declined over the past century or so and most of the CO_2 emitted accumulates in the atmosphere and remains there for hundreds of years.

Accurate and direct measurements of atmospheric CO_2 are taken at the Mauna Loa Observatory in Hawaii, which began in earnest in 1958. The early measurements at this site confirmed that atmospheric CO_2 had risen to about 315 parts per million (ppm), an increase of just 35 ppm in the 150 years or so since the onset of the industrial revolution. However, the concentration measured rose significantly in the next 70 years, to about 420 ppm in 2022. To put this into context, a person born in 1950 would have seen an increase of over 30% in atmospheric CO_2, or 100 ppm, in their lifetime. As indicated above, this level of atmospheric CO_2 has not been seen for a million years and is set to continue to rise for much of this century, even with a strong decarbonisation response by the global community. Perhaps most worrying is the fact that two major recent perturbations to the world system – the 2008 financial crisis and the COVID pandemic – have had little effect on the inexorable rise in atmospheric CO_2.

The atmospheric concentrations of the other main contributing greenhouse gases – CH_4, N_2O, and SF_6 – are also rising. Sources of CH_4 include emissions from fossil fuel production and leakage during its transport, sometimes over very long distances; other major sources include the emission from the decay of organic matter in wetlands, including rice production, and from ruminant animals such as cows. The lifetime of CH_4 in the atmosphere is relatively short, at about 12 years. N_2O sources include agriculture, fuel combustion, wastewater management, and industrial processes; it has an estimated lifetime in the atmosphere of about 115 years. SF_6, a very stable chemical with a lifetime of 3,200 years, is used in electrical transmission and distribution equipment, the manufacture of electronics, and the production of aluminium and magnesium. Underpinning all these emissions is the economic development of a growing global population.

The recorded concentration of CH_4 has risen from 1,645 parts per billion (ppb) in 1984 to 1,912 ppb in 2022; that for N_2O has risen from 316 ppb in 2001 to 336 ppb in 2022; and that for SF_6 from just over 4 parts per trillion (ppt) in 1995 to about 11 ppt in 2022. Although these concentrations are much lower than those for CO_2, their Global Warming Potential (GWP) is much higher: CH_4 is about 20 times more potent than CO_2 as a greenhouse agent over a one-century timescale, while N_2O and SF_6 are about 300 and 24,000 times more effective than CO_2, respectively, over the same timescale. Reducing the emission of these gases is also an important activity in addressing climate change.

1.4 Global temperatures

The average global temperature has also been rising. When compared to the 20th-century average, the observed temperature has been consistently warmer in the period 1980–2022; this contrasts with observed temperatures in the period 1880–1935 which were consistently colder when compared to the same average. The size of these temperature 'anomalies' is also significant: they are now almost 1°C above the average in the most recent period, compared with a maximum of 0.5°C below the average in the earlier period. The warmest years on record have been recorded over the past decade, and this has once again prompted a call for action to limit average global temperatures to 1.5°C by 2050.

Climate change is a complex issue, and its manifestations are many. Some are small scale, regional in nature, and relatively short-lived such as extreme weather events; others are much larger scale, more dramatic, and longer lasting, such as droughts and aridification. There is also the possibility of what are irreversible events, at least on the human timescale, such as melting of the polar icecaps and weakening of the Atlantic Meridional Overturn Current (AMOC). The latter circulates water from north to south and back in a long cycle within the Atlantic Ocean, bringing warmth to various parts of the world; it also carries nutrients vital to ocean life.

Recent research shows that the AMOC has weakened by about 15% compared to historic norms, brought about by increased rainfall in the North Atlantic resulting from global warming (and evaporation) in the tropics; this has the effect of reducing ocean water density and altering the flow of the current. The North Atlantic is cooling, and many countries, in Northern Europe, for example, will experience much cooler temperatures while in other parts of the world, temperatures will be higher.

Most concerning is that if this process continues, there is an increasing likelihood that it will reach a tipping point where it may 'switch off' completely. The last time the AMOC 'shut down' was towards the end of the last ice age, about 14,500 years ago. Then glacial melt flooded the North Atlantic with freshwater, altering the salinity of ocean water and collapsing the system, causing temperatures in Europe to fall significantly.

1.5 Global response to climate change

No part of the earth is immune from the effects of climate change. Renewed efforts to reduce greenhouse gas emissions will help lessen the impacts of this phenomenon, but people will also have to learn to adapt to their new environment. This is not a new prospect, as evidenced by the many sites around the world that now lie abandoned and lost to history following changed environmental circumstances. People, then, have had to adapt to dramatic changes in their environment, perhaps through the adoption of new technology and practices or, in extreme cases, by migrating to regions less affected. But the scale of the problem and the implications for the populations involved are much greater than before, making some options more difficult than in the past.

The Paris Agreement was a seminal Conference of the Parties (COP) held in 2015 and is a legally binding international treaty on climate change. It was adopted by 196 Parties and entered into force in 2016. Its goal is to limit global warming to well below 2°C, preferably to 1.5°C, compared to pre-industrial levels. The Agreement works on a five-year cycle of increasingly ambitious climate action carried out by countries. The latter were required to submit their plans for action in the form of Nationally Determined Contributions (NDCs) by 2020. In their NDCs, countries outline actions they will take to reduce their greenhouse gas emissions to reach the goals of the Paris Agreement. Also, countries suggest the actions they will take to build resilience and to adapt to the impacts of rising temperatures.

The 2020s decade is a crucial one for action on climate change, requiring a step-change reduction in greenhouse gas emissions if the world is to avoid the effects of rising global temperatures. It was, then, important that the 26th Conference of the Parties (COP26) in Glasgow signal that countries are serious about meeting their 2030 obligations under the Paris Agreement. It was also important that there was recognition of the need to go further and sooner if average global temperatures are to be limited to no more than 2.0°C and preferably 1.5°C above pre-industrial levels, as agreed in Paris.

The COP26 agreement, the Glasgow Climate Pact, suggested some progress was made, particularly in four key areas: CH_4 emissions, the use of coal, deforestation, and financial support for poorer countries impacted by climate change. As indicated above, CH_4 is a particularly damaging greenhouse gas, and the Pact set a 30% reduction target in CH_4 emissions by 2030; this was signed by over 100 countries, although three major emitters – China, Russia, and India – did not. Coal featured in a COP agreement for the first time with a pledge to phase down (not phase out) its use, although no timescale was suggested and two key coal users – China and India – were reluctant to support stronger measures at this time due to their heavy reliance on this fuel.

Deforestation has been a major concern for decades. Well over 100 countries accounting for 85% of the world's forests, agreed to stop deforestation by 2030. Crucially, Brazil, the custodian of the vast Amazonian Forest, was one of signatories, and their action on this issue will be closely scrutinised over the coming years. The thorny question of financial support for developing countries was raised, and there was agreement to increase the money to help the poorer nations to adapt to climate change. Despite a previous $100 billion a year commitment by 2020 not being met, the richer countries pledged to increase financial support for these countries.

These were good outcomes, so long as nations follow through on their pledges, yet some people have questioned the value of the annual COP process. Tens of thousands of people participated in COP26, and the media coverage was extensive. There is no doubt that it raised awareness of the climate change issue, bringing it into people's homes and encouraging discussion, as do all the COPs. There was also considerable 'direct' action by activists who believe that climate change is an existential issue that requires much more action from decision-makers in governments, industry, and other organisations, and there were some people who simply thought this was a wasted exercise.

The evidence that the COP process can deliver the level of greenhouse gas emission reduction needed to stabilise the climate over the next three decades is not promising, judging by the latest levels of CO_2 measured in the atmosphere. At first sight, this may suggest that the COP process has not been effective, but it is likely that CO_2 levels in the atmosphere would have been higher in the absence of an international process. However, the key point is that the COP process is not as effective as it needs to be, and it is important this is addressed.

A major new initiative at COP26 gives a clue as to what needs to happen alongside this formal process. As indicated above, China and the United States were the two largest CO_2 emitters in 2020; they have also been the largest emitters, cumulatively, in the period 1965–2020. It was encouraging, then, that they reported they had been in bilateral discussions on climate change and had agreed to work together over the next decade to help achieve the target set out in the Paris Agreement. This was a very important initiative, assuming there is meaningful follow-through with action, because these countries are not only the two major emitters but also the two largest economies in the world and fierce commercial competitors. Encouragingly, it does suggest a way forward whereby the largest emitters in the world can and should collaborate outside the formal COP process; the potential benefits to the world are huge.

Interestingly, there are forums whereby these countries can come together and agree to act on climate change, unencumbered by the need to reach a consensus with a much larger number of countries that attend the COPs and away from the glare of the media and the public. For example, five of the highest emitting countries – United States, Japan, Germany, the United Kingdom, and Canada – are members of the Group of 7 (G7) major economies; perhaps more importantly, these countries along with China, Russia, India, and Brazil, are members of the G20. This, then, offers ample opportunity for countries to discuss climate mitigation measures alongside the thorny issues of trade, competition, and financial support for poorer countries.

The climate is changing, and the evidence that we are entering a more challenging period continues to grow. Global land-sea temperatures reported show a steady increase over the past 50 years; the temperature increase is currently almost 1°C higher than the average temperature in the period 1950–1980. These record global temperatures have resulted in shrinking polar ice sheets and rising sea levels, extreme weather, including intense storms, and more frequent droughts and wildfires. Water resources are affected: in some areas, too much rainfall in a short time causes floods, while in other parts of the world, too little rainfall is putting enormous strain on freshwater resources. The latter is projected to get much worse in the future as temperatures continue to rise through 2050.

1.6 Climate change implications for water resources

Concerns around the impacts of climate change have centred on rising temperatures and changing weather patterns, evidenced by highly visible short-term events such as wildfires, intense storms, and flooding; their effects have been devastating, with considerable physical destruction to the environment and significant loss of human life. Longer term drought conditions and the availability of water have received less attention, yet the figures are alarming, with a significant portion of the world population lacking access to clean freshwater for some periods during the year.

The United Nations estimates that global water use has increased by a factor of six over the past 100 years and continues to grow at a rate of about 1% per year. Available surface water resources at the continent level remain relatively constant but many countries are already experiencing water scarcity conditions. Almost all countries in a belt around 10°–40° North, from Mexico to China, including Southern Europe, are affected by water scarcity, together with Australia, Western South America, and Southern Africa in the Southern Hemisphere.

It is perhaps strange to be worried about water resources when over 70% of the world's surface is covered by water. However, the freshwater resources on which we rely make up just 3% of the total, and most of this, being ice, is not readily accessible. The World Bank reports the estimated annual freshwater withdrawals as a percentage of the freshwater renewals by country. A simple analysis shows that the average value of withdrawals has risen from around 50% in 1992 using the available data from 120 countries to almost 70% covering 178 countries in 2018; there are a significant number of countries exceeding 100%.

The United Nations suggests that water scarcity occurs when annual freshwater withdrawals amount to greater than 25% of the renewable water resources; on this basis, 60 countries around the world currently suffer from water scarcity. A more granular analysis is possible by considering three bands: those countries that do not suffer from water stress are those in which annual freshwater withdrawals amount to less than 20% of the renewable water; countries suffer from water scarcity or severe water scarcity if withdrawals amount to 20–40% and greater than 40% of renewable resources, respectively. Using the most recent World Bank data available, 43 countries suffered severe water shortages in 2018 and 27 suffered water shortages; the remaining 108 countries have freshwater supplies to meet their current needs.

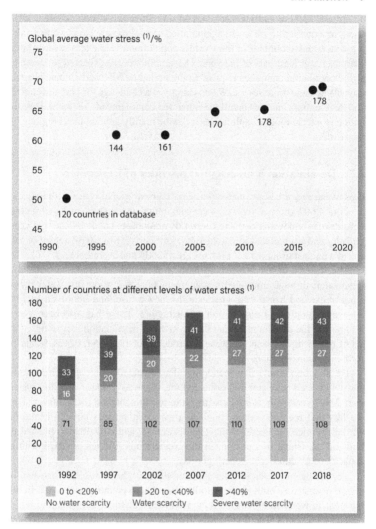

Figure 1.2 Level of water stress increasing across the world

Source: World Development Indicators, World Bank, 2022.

Note: (1), Level of water stress is defined as freshwater withdrawal as a proportion of available freshwater resources.

Crucially, these metrics mean that an estimated two billion people world-wide, or a quarter of the world's population, do not have access to safe drinking water, and about half of the world's population experiences severe water scarcity for at least part of the year. These numbers are expected to increase as the population continues to grow in the period to 2050 and climate change impacts become more severe. Water scarcity is a challenge for both developed and developing countries on all the inhabited continents of the world. Desalination is a technological solution that can be readily applied in all regions of the world.

1.7 Desalination is an essential provider of freshwater

Freshwater resources are under pressure. Current global water withdrawals, at about 4,600 km^3 per year, are near maximum sustainable levels, while the volume of groundwater extracted currently amounts to about 960 km^3 per year globally and is predicted to rise to 1,100 km^3 per year by 2050; a third of the world's biggest groundwater systems are already under pressure.

The water industry is working hard to meet the increasing demand for freshwater: through improved management of water resources, water recycling, reuse and harvesting, greater efficiency in use, and improvements in the water supply and distribution infrastructure. There has also been good progress in the development and deployment of desalination technology, the act of removing salt from saltwater to produce potable water, that is, water fit for human consumption.

Desalination is not a new technology, having been exploited by Greek sailors who boiled saltwater and collected the steam to produce drinking water over 2,000 years ago; sailors continued to use this method for centuries. The world's first recorded commercial desalination plant was built in Malta in 1881 to service the needs of the Tigne barracks, and a distillation plant was built on the island of Curaçao, in the Netherlands Antilles, in 1928 with a capacity of 60 cubic metres (m^3) per day.

Technological developments gathered pace. In the 1930s, the first desalination plants were built in the Middle East. These countries were rich in oil but poor in water resources, so they used their newfound oil wealth to build desalination plants. The first Multi-Effect Distillation (MED) plant was built in Saudi Arabia; this technology involved a low-temperature thermal process of obtaining freshwater by recovering the vapour of boiling seawater, not un-like the Greek sailors two thousand years earlier but using much more efficient technology and on a larger scale.

The 1950s also saw some significant developments: The United States Congress passed *The Saline Water Act* in 1952 to provide federal support for desalination, and the first Multi-Stage Flash Distillation (MSF) plant was built in Kuwait in 1957. In this technology, hot water was stored at low pressure in

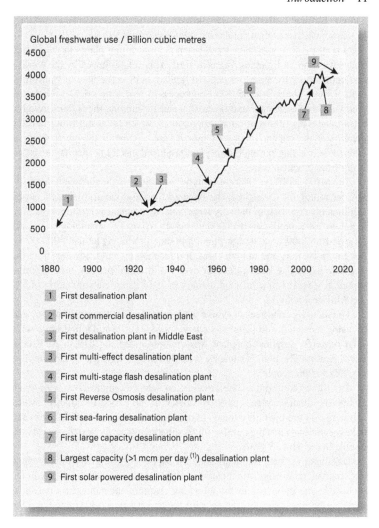

Figure 1.3 Milestones in the development of desalination

Sources: Freshwater Data from Water Use and Stress, Our World in Data, 2018; Milestones from Desalination Plant History, Preceden, and Does Size Matter? Meet Ten of the World's Largest Desalination Plants, Aquatech, 2021.

Note: (1), mcm is million cubic metres.

a large chamber, with the low pressure causing the water to change instantly to steam, which was then condensed into drinking water.

One of the first seawater desalination demonstration plants in the United States was built at Freeport, Texas in 1961. This was followed by the world's first commercial Reverse Osmosis (RO) plant, built in the state of California, in the United States in 1965. RO is a process of removing salt and other contaminants from saltwater and brackish water by running the water through a membrane with 1,000s of microscopic pores. When the water flows into the membrane, the salt and other contaminants are captured in the pores, with potable water passing through. This plant produced just 22 m^3 per day of freshwater from brackish water.

The MED, MSF, and RO concepts are now the three mainstream desalination technologies. Over time, the scale of the desalination plants increased significantly. The first of the very large capacity plants was built in Ashkelon, Israel, in 2005, producing 165,000 m^3 per day using RO technology; this was followed in 2009 by a similar plant, this time producing almost 400,000 m^3 per day in Hadera, and in both cases, RO technology and feedwater from the sea were used. The largest plant of over 1 million m^3 per day, was commissioned at Ras Al Kahir in Saudi Arabia in 2014 using a combination of RO and MSF technologies.

The industry continues to evolve, both in terms of scale and efficiency and by using renewables to supply its energy needs. The world's first large scale solar-powered desalination plant was commissioned in 2017 in Al Khafji, Saudi Arabia. The plant's capacity is 60,000 m^3 per day, enough to supply a city of 150,000 people.

The global footprint of the desalination sector is impressive, with about 20,000 desalination plants built worldwide in the period to 2020, of which about 16,000 are operating today. Many more are planned in the future, and the expectation is that the number of desalination plants around the world may double in the next 25 years.

Desalination, then, is a major industry supported by a global supply chain but receives relatively little attention compared to, say, developments in the renewable energy sector. In the following chapters, the context for desalination will be discussed, beginning with the drivers of water demand and the natural water resources available. The desalination technologies will be described and the attributes of the 'winning' technologies highlighted. Energy and environmental impacts are key issues for the sector, and these are discussed along with possible future developments in these areas.

The role that desalination plays in ten country case studies in water-scarce regions of the world is discussed and serves to explore different dimensions of the technology. The further evolution of this sector in water provision in the period to 2050 and the environmental consequences are explored using scenario analysis.

Summary key points

- Climate change is the defining issue of the 21st century and will make the world much more challenging. Governments and the water industry around the world will need to address increasing water scarcity and the provision of potable water.

- The greenhouse effect associated with our atmosphere is a natural phenomenon that has kept the earth's environment stable and habitable for thousands of years.

- Human activity has led to rising concentrations of greenhouse agents – CO_2, CH_4, N_2O, and SF_6 – enhancing the greenhouse effect. This is leading to higher global temperatures and changes in climate patterns around the world.

- The evidence that our climate is changing is clear and predictable – an increasing frequency and scale of extreme weather events, longer droughts, and greater aridification – but efforts so far have been less than needed to limit rising global temperatures.

- Climate change requires action in the form of mitigation to limit the scale of the problem and adaptation in those regions that are already or will be under considerable stress in the coming years and decades.

- Water resources in some regions are already under extreme pressure, made worse by climate change. Better management of renewable resources, innovation, and new technologies will help alleviate the problem.

- Desalination is an important technology that has emerged in the mainstream water industry over the last few decades. It is playing a very important role in water-stressed regions around the world, relieving pressure on renewable and groundwater resources.

2 Water resources

The consumption of freshwater has grown enormously over the last 100 years due to a rapid growth in global population and economic development, and this has placed enormous pressure on available freshwater resources.

2.1 Global growth in water consumption

In the last chapter, it was noted that global water use increased by a factor of six over the past 100 years and continues to grow at a rate of about 1% per year; at this average rate, water consumption will increase by a further 35% in the period 2020–2050. Demand is driven by several factors, including population growth, economic development, and changing consumption patterns; to these must be added climate change, which will serve to exacerbate the problem throughout this century.

Innovation and new technologies will help ensure the security of water supply going forward, and consumer behaviour will also play an important role in the more efficient use of water. Better water management in the domestic, industrial, and business sectors will mean less pressure on water resources than would otherwise be the case. However, the indications are that despite such progress, water resources will come under greater pressure, and for many countries, potable water from desalination will play an increasingly important role with larger and more efficient plants deployed in the future.

2.1.1 Social, economic, and environmental drivers of water demand

The demand for clean water provision is now enshrined in the United Nations (UN) Sustainable Development Goals (SDGs). SDG6 refers directly to water, highlighting the need to *ensure the availability and sustainable management of water and sanitation for all.* Several of the other SDGs also rely on the ready availability of freshwater. For example, the SDG2 objective is to *end hunger, achieve food security and improved nutrition and promote sustainable*

DOI: 10.4324/9781003334224-2

agriculture, while the SDG3 focus is to *ensure healthy lives and promote well-being for all at all ages;* to achieve these SDGs, it requires plentiful and secure supplies of freshwater. In a broader context, the provision of utilities such as water, energy, and communications are all important for SDG11, which seeks to *make cities and human settlements inclusive, safe, resilient, and sustainable.*

Social drivers

Population, directly and indirectly, has, arguably, been the single largest driver of water demand. The global population 2000 years ago was estimated at around 230 million, a number reached after 10,000 years of human development. The time taken to double the global population has since fallen dramatically: 1,400 years the first time, 380 years the second time, 135 years the third time, and 57 years the fourth time, so that by 1972 the population was 3.82 billion; the population doubled again just 48 years later in 2020 to 7.84 billion. This is an astonishing outcome, brought about by the increased availability of food and water, the development of medicines and the eradication of diseases, and the development of new technology to aid human activities. These have led to declining death rates among the young, particularly in developing countries, and extended average lifetimes for the old; it is now not uncommon for people in the developed nations to live into their 80s.

In terms of geographical distribution, Asia had the largest population in 2020, at just under 60% of the world total; China and India were the most populous, each contributing around 18% of the total. In terms of age distribution, Asia has 24% of its population below the age of 15 and just 10% over the age of 65. Europe and Africa are at different ends of the population spectrum. Europe, which contributes 10% of the world population, has a markedly different distribution: just 16% of its population is under the age of 15, while almost 20% are over the age of 65. Africa contributes 17% to the world population, with an age distribution of 40% below the age of 15 and just 3% above the age of 65.

The inexorable rise in the world population shows some signs of slowing down. A recent report suggests that the world population will peak at about 9 billion before the middle of the century, much lower than had previously been reported, and then begin to decline; the peak date could come sooner by raising average incomes and education levels. This will have implications for economic activity and the related issues of energy and environment, and there will continue to be considerable stress on water resources in many heavily populated regions of the world.

In addition to a major increase in population, there has been a mass movement of people from rural to urban centres. About 200 years ago, just 3% of the world's population lived in cities, but industrialisation encouraged people to move to the cities. In 1960, the urban population was estimated at about

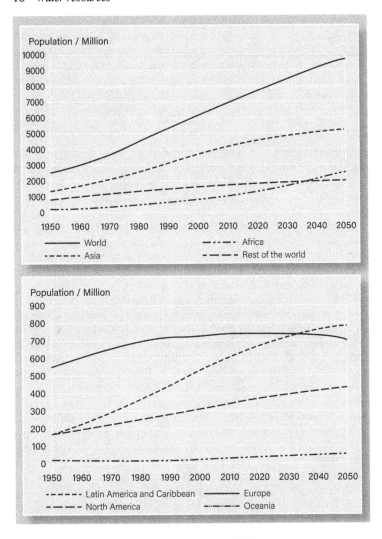

Figure 2.1 Inexorable rise in population to the middle of the century

Source: Population Trends 1950–2100 Globally and within Europe, European Environment Agency, 2021.

Note: Lower chart has an expanded y-scale.

1 billion, or one-third of the global population, and 50 years later, the number increased to 50% of a much larger global population. Estimates of people living in cities differ depending on the definition of what constitutes an urban conurbation, but today there are more people living in cities than in rural environments, and there are many very large cities, the largest of which is Tokyo, with a population of over 37 million. This transition has increased demand for energy, food, and water.

Human development, then, is linked to access to safe drinking water. The evidence for this is a strong correlation between a country's Human Development Index (HDI) and the percentage of people in the country with access to safe drinking water. The HDI measures a country's progress in three areas of human development: health, education, and standard of living. Health is measured as the life expectancy at birth, while education is a composite of expected years and the average number of years spent in education; the standard of living is given as the Gross National Income (GNI) per capita (currently expressed in $2017 based on purchasing power parity).

A country's HDI is calculated from the geometric mean of these three dimensions for each country. There are four HDI categories: low human development for those countries where the HDI value is <0.55, medium human development where the value is in the range 0.550–0.699, high human development for the range 0.700–0.799, and very high development for those countries with a value >0.800. The most recent United Nations Development Programme (UNDP) Report shows there are 32 countries with the lowest HDI value and 44 with medium human development; there are 49 and 66 countries in the high and very high HDI value categories, respectively.

Encouragingly, the global HDI has increased significantly over the last 30 years, from 0.60 to about 0.75 in 2019, falling back slightly to 0.73 in 2021 due to the COVID pandemic. Over this period, a significant number of countries have moved up from one HDI category to another, and there is an expectation that this will continue in the coming decades. Access to safe drinking water is an important contributor to this transition.

Economic drivers

Economic activity is made up of four main groups: primary, secondary, tertiary, and quaternary activity. Primary activity refers to the extraction of raw materials from the earth, with farming being the most important activity in this group; other activities in this group include mining, fishing, and forestry. All these activities involve extracting materials from land and water. Secondary activity is the processing of these raw materials into useful products, from small-scale cottage industries to large-scale commercial businesses. Tertiary activity involves the sale of manufactured goods, while quaternary activity involves the provision of information services such as education, and research and development, consultation, health services, and entertainment.

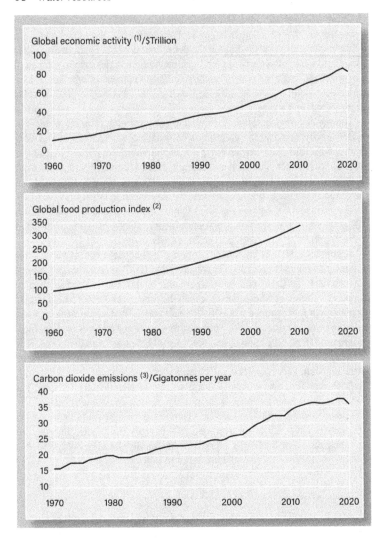

Figure 2.2 Economic, social, and environmental drivers for water consumption

Sources: (1), World Development Indicators, World Bank, 2022 (Units in $2015); (2), How we feed the world today, OECD (Index relative to 100 in 1960); (3), Climate Change 2022: Mitigation of Climate Change, Working Group III contribution to the Sixth Assessment Report of the Intergovernmental Panel on Climate Change, 2022.

Economic activity has grown in sympathy with population growth. This is not surprising since each of the four groups that contribute to economic activity involves people, to a lesser or greater extent depending on the level of development and the activity involved. In the 60-year period from 1960 to 2020, the population grew by a factor of 2.6, from 3 billion to 7.6 billion people; economic activity grew by a factor of 8 over the same period, from $10 trillion (in $2015) to $80 trillion.

Agriculture is the major consumer of water. Global food production grew by a factor of 3.3 in the period 1960–2015 in sympathy with the growth in the world's population. The industry benefited from a 'green' revolution that involved increasing the area of land for food production, using higher-yielding crop strains or seeds, and improving the yield output by using fertilisers, pesticides, and herbicides; to these must be added the use of equipment and improving farming practices, including irrigation.

As with energy, the global connectivity associated with agriculture benefits people across the world, helping to alleviate food poverty. This connectivity is robust to some shocks and not to others. For example, an unexpected ramification of the war in Ukraine, which began in 2022, was the impact on grain exports from the country, the so-called 'breadbasket' of Europe but also an important supplier of grain and other food products to countries around the world. It required an agreement to allow shipments to pass through the Black Sea while the war continued, to avert a catastrophe in some African countries. A war in one region that lasts a long time places a strain on food production and the associated freshwater supplies elsewhere.

Economic activity, then, leads to a better quality of life for people, from the provision of shelter, food, and clean water to an increase in spending power on goods, services, and leisure activities. However, economic activity also consumes resources, including freshwater, and this is becoming a major challenge in many parts of the world.

Environmental drivers

Climate change and its implications for freshwater resources were discussed in Chapter 1. Briefly, the underlying process leading to climate change is relatively straightforward: the atmosphere contains carbon dioxide (CO_2) and other gases such as water, methane (CH_4), and nitrous oxide (N_2O), and their concentrations were relatively stable for thousands of years leading up to the industrial revolution. These gases are 'greenhouse' agents, and as such, their radiative properties helped to keep the earth's atmosphere and surface temperature at a level that was suitable for ecosystems across the world. However, increasing the concentration of greenhouse gases in the atmosphere leads to greater 'radiative forcing' and thus higher global temperatures; the latter naturally leads to changing weather patterns.

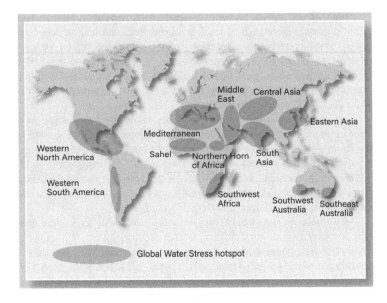

Figure 2.3 Many regions experiencing high water stress

Source: 2021 State of Climate Services: Water, World Meteorological Organisation, 2021.

Notes: Water stress occurs when the demand for water exceeds the available amount during a certain period or when poor quality restricts its use; Southwest Australia added by the author.

There are natural sources of the main greenhouse gases except synthetic chemicals such as sulphur hexafluoride (SF_6). However, the rising global population and the associated economic activity are having a profound impact on the natural environment. Economic and social activity is underpinned by energy consumption in transport, electricity generation, and industrial production. Nearly all the energy has been provided by fossil fuels since the industrial revolution, initially by coal in the 19th century, followed by oil and gas in the 20th century. Their production, transport, and use have produced enormous quantities of carbon dioxide (CO_2), and to a lesser extent, methane, that have been emitted into the atmosphere.

The climate change phenomenon will affect human and animal welfare profoundly, bringing many new challenges, including the sustainable provision of freshwater supplies (Figure 2.3).

2.1.2 Demand for freshwater

Chapter 1 highlighted concern around the impacts of climate change, with rising temperatures and changing weather patterns evidenced by highly visible short-term events such as wildfires, intense storms, and flooding. Longer-term drought conditions, aridification, and the availability of water have received less attention, yet the figures are alarming. The UN estimates that about 1.9 billion people, or about a quarter of the global population, live in severely water-scarce areas, and about 3.6 billion people worldwide are already living in potential water-scarce areas for short periods each year.

Water consumption

As indicated above, the consumption of water has grown enormously over the last 100 years, brought about by a growing population and increased economic activity. The availability of water has been an issue in many parts of the world, affecting billions of people to a lesser or greater degree. But it is fair to say that the onset of climate change is making water scarcity even more acute in those areas and this is set to continue as climate change impacts become more prevalent in the coming decades.

Water consumption has grown from about 670 billion m^3 (or 670 km^3) in 1,900 to over 4,000 billion m^3 or 4,000 km^3 today, an increase by a factor of six; current global water withdrawals, then, are near maximum sustainable levels. The use of groundwater currently amounts to about 800 km^3 per year globally and is predicted to rise to 1,100 km^3 per year by 2050. A third of the world's biggest groundwater systems are already under pressure.

The regional consumption of water has remained the same over the last century. By far the largest regional consumers today are the countries in Asia, and these amount to about 60% of the total; this is perhaps not surprising since this region contains the two most populous countries in the world, China and India. The developed countries of North America and Europe consume just under 17% and 12%, respectively, while developing countries in South America and Africa consume just over 5% and 6%, respectively; Australia and Oceania consume the least, at just 1% of the total.

Agriculture dominates water consumption in countries around the world. The global average freshwater withdrawal for agriculture as a percentage of total freshwater withdrawals is just over 71% today, but this value varies significantly depending on each country's circumstances; some developing countries, for example, have a value > 90% while smaller developed nations have a value of <1%. The global average freshwater withdrawal for industry is just under 17% of the total, and once again, this varies significantly across countries; in this case, it is the most developed countries that consume at higher levels, with the least developed countries having little industrial activity. The domestic sector average is the lowest at 12%, and here the size of the population and the economic and social circumstances of each country play a role in determining the contribution this sector makes to the total withdrawals.

2.1.3   Key drivers in selected countries

In Chapter 5, a set of ten country case studies is presented that explore different aspects of desalination. The countries chosen lie in regions where water scarcity is an issue and desalination technologies have been deployed: Saudi Arabia, Israel, and Morocco in the Middle East and North Africa (MENA); Spain, Cyprus, and the UK in Europe; the USA and Chile in North and South America, respectively; China in the Asia region; and Australia in Oceania. The social, economic, and climate indicators discussed above provide an important context for the desalination sector in these countries today and in the future, and Table 2.1 below presents a few of these indicators.

Population growth has significant implications for water resources. The population in the countries selected covers a large range, from just over a million in the island state of Cyprus to 1.4 billion in China. Two countries have projected stable populations over the next decade, while several countries continue to grow at more than 1% per annum. For example, an average 1.4% per annum growth in Saudi Arabia means the population will rise from 36 million to 38.6 million in this short period. In terms of the UN's HDI, Morocco is classified as a medium human development country, while China

Table 2.1 Social, economic, and extreme weather indicators in selected countries

Continent	Country	Population In 2021/ Million[1]	Average annual population growth for 2020–25/ % per year[2]	HDI[3]	GDP per capita in 2021/ $US[4]	CRI score for 2000– 2019[5], [6]
Middle East	Saudi Arabia	36.0	1.4	0.875	25586	100
	Israel	9.4	1.5	0.919	51430	120
North Africa	Morocco	37.1	1.1	0.683	3497	96
Europe	Spain	47.4	− 0.1	0.909	30116	47
	Cyprus	1.2	0.6[7]	0.896	30799	130
	UK	67.3	0.4	0.929	47334	65
North America	USA	331.9	0.6	0.921	69286	n/a
South America	Chile	19.5	0.1	0.858	16503	81
Asia	China	1412.4	0.3	0.768	12556	56
Oceania	Australia	25.7	1.1	0.951	59934	48

Sources: (1), World Bank, 2022; (2), The Economist in Numbers, 2022; (3), Human Development Index, UNDP, 2022; (4), Gross Domestic Product, World Bank, 2022; (5), Global Climate Risk Index 2021, David Eckstein et al., Germanwatch Institute, 2021; (6), Impacts of extreme weather events and the socio-economic losses caused in 182 countries in the period 2000–2019.

Note: (7), Estimated, World Bank 2022; n/a, not available. GDP, Gross Domestic Product; HDI, Human Development Index; CRI, Climate Risk Index.

is seen as a high development country; the other eight countries in the case study set are in the highest band of development.

Water produced by desalination can be expensive, and a country's economic strength will play a role in the extent of deployment possible. The economic well-being, then, of the countries chosen varies significantly, with a Gross Domestic Product (GDP) per capita of just under $US 3,500 in Morocco to almost $US 70,000 in the USA.

There is increasing evidence that extreme weather events are linked to the onset of climate change. The Global Climate Risk Index (CRI) is a helpful metric and reflects the number of fatalities and economic losses that arise from extreme events such as heatwaves, storms, and floods; however, it does not consider the gradual, longer-term impacts of climate change such as drought and aridification, melting glaciers, and sea level rise.

The CRI methodology uses a country's ranking within the 180 countries considered for each of four factors – fatalities, fatalities per unit of population, economic losses, and economic losses per unit of GDP – and a simple formula with appropriate weightings to calculate the index: the lower the index the more at risk the country is from extreme weather events. The most affected country over the period 2000–2019 in the world is the island of Puerto Rico in the Caribbean, with a CRI score of just 7, while the least affected is Qatar, with a score of 173. Of the countries in the case study set shown in Table 2.1, Spain, with a CRI score of 47, has been the most affected by extreme weather events over the last 20 years, while Cyprus is the least affected, with a score of 130.

2.2   Water resources

Water stress occurs when the demand for water exceeds the available amount during a certain period or when poor quality restricts its use. Available surface water resources at continent level remain relatively constant, but many countries are already experiencing water scarcity conditions. Almost all countries in a belt around 10°–40° North, from Mexico to China, including Southern Europe, are affected by water scarcity, together with Australia, Western South America, and Southern Africa in the Southern Hemisphere.

The level of water stress in any country is reported as freshwater withdrawals as a proportion of available freshwater resources. There are various levels of water stress: extremely high if the ratio of withdrawals to supply is >80%; high if the ratio is between 40 and 80%; medium-to-high for a ratio between 20 and 40%; low-to-medium if the ratio is between 10 and 20%; and low if the ratio is <10%. The number of countries around the world that fell into the >80% category in 2018 was 24 (out of 178 that reported this indicator); 19 countries fell into the 40–80% category, 27 countries in the 20–40% category, 22 countries in the 10–20% category, and 86 countries in the <10% category.

The UN has a simpler definition: *When a territory withdraws 25 per cent or more of its renewable freshwater resources it is said to be 'water-stressed'.*

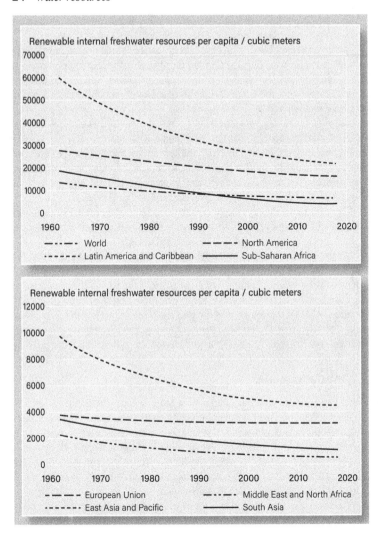

Figure 2.4 Decline in water resources across the world

Source: World Development Indicators, The World Bank, 2022.

Note: Lower chart has an expanded y-scale.

If this definition is used, then 60 countries around the world were water-stressed in 2018. Perhaps most worrying is the fact that 16 countries are withdrawing over 100% of their renewable resources; the Middle East and North Africa MENA region is home to 12 of these countries, with just four countries beyond: Uzbekistan, Turkmenistan, Sudan, and Pakistan.

It is perhaps strange to suggest there is scarcity on a planet where just over 70% of the surface is covered with water, albeit almost all to saltwater. The total volume of water on earth is estimated at 1,410 million km³; to put this into context, this volume would make a single, spherical drop with a radius of just 693 km, the distance between Paris and Munich in Europe. The oceans, seas, and bays account for over 96.5% of the total water resources on earth; ice caps, glaciers, and permanent snow contain 1.7%; and groundwater sources account for a further 1.7%. Together, these three sources alone account for very close to 100% of the earth's water resources.

The total freshwater resources are estimated to be 35 million km³, and in this case, the volume could be contained in a spherical drop with a radius of just over 137 km, which is about the same as the distance between Qatar and Bahrain in the Middle East. Most of the freshwater is contained in two sources: 69% is in the form of ice caps, glaciers, and permanent snow, and 30% is contained in groundwater sources. There are several smaller but important contributions: 0.86% is contained in ground ice and permafrost, 0.26% in lakes, and just under 0.04% in swamps and rivers; moisture in the atmosphere and in the soil are estimated at 0.4% and 0.5% of the total freshwater, respectively.

There is, then, about 13,000 km³ in the form of water vapour in the atmosphere, and if this fell as precipitation at once, the Earth would be covered with only about 2.5 cm of water. Weather patterns, however, ensure that rain falls in a very uneven way over land and sea, sometimes sparsely and at other times torrentially; and it is increasingly evident that the weather and rainfall patterns are changing due to the impacts of climate change.

2.2.1 Freshwater resources

Internal freshwater resources refer, in the main, to river flows and groundwater; renewable internal resources are those replenished by rainfall. Several indicators are available to help describe the scale and use of renewable water resources in a country, and these indicators help provide a context for the development of the desalination sector in each country. The World Bank defines the following four key indicators:

1) Level of water stress or water (in %): *The level of water stress is the freshwater withdrawal as a proportion of available freshwater resources.* Regions are considered water scarce when total annual withdrawals for human use are between 20 and 40% of the total available renewable surface water resources, and severely water scarce when withdrawals exceed 40%.

2) Annual freshwater withdrawals, total (in billion cubic meters): Annual freshwater withdrawals refer to *total water withdrawals, not counting evaporation losses from storage basins*; withdrawals also include water from desalination plants.

3) Annual freshwater withdrawals (in % of internal resources): *Total water withdrawals, not counting evaporation losses from storage basins*; withdrawals also include water from desalination plants. Withdrawals can exceed 100 percent of total renewable resources where extraction from non-renewable aquifers or supply by desalination plants is considerable or where there is significant water reuse.

4) Renewable internal freshwater resources per capita (in cubic metres, m^3): *internal renewable resources (internal river flows and groundwater from rainfall) in the country.*

At the global level, internal freshwater resources have largely remained unchanged over the last 60 years or so and are estimated to be about 42.5 trillion m^3 each year. As indicated above, the population has risen dramatically over this period, from just over 3 billion to 8 billion. This increase in population set against the constant internal renewable resources means the global per capita value has fallen from just over 13,000 m^3 to about 5,500 m^3 in this period; the pressure on renewable resources, then, will increase throughout this century as the population and economic activity increase further.

Freshwater resources at the regional level

There are major regional differences in internal freshwater resources per capita. In 1960, Latin America enjoyed a value of over 60,000 m^3, while North America had a value of just under half that value. Sub-Saharan Africa and the East Asia and Pacific region were also reasonably well endowed with per capita values of just under 20,000 m^3 and 10,000 m^3, respectively. The European Union and the populous South Asia region had relatively low per capita values of about 4,000 m^3, while the MENA region had just half this value.

Not surprisingly, the downward trend in global per capita values is repeated across nearly all the regions in the world. Latin America has seen a fall by about a factor of three since 1960, while North America per capita resources have declined by about a factor of two; the Sub-Saharan region has seen the largest decline, falling by over a factor of four. The East Asia and Pacific region, South Asia region, and MENA regions have also seen a significant decline in per capita resources, and this from low values in 1960; the per capita value in the European Union has remained broadly the same over the last 60 years, reflecting the needs of more mature economic development and a relatively stable population.

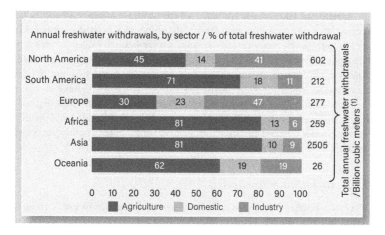

Figure 2.5 Freshwater withdrawals by region and sector

Source: Groundwater. Making the Invisible Visible, The United Nations World Water Development Report, 2022.

Note: Data are for 2017; one billion m³ is one km³.

There are significant regional differences in terms of the absolute volume of freshwater available, the level of annual replenishment of these resources, and water withdrawals. Table 2.2 shows that Asia, Africa, and North America are well-endowed with freshwater resources; South America, Europe, and Oceania are less so. However, South America has the largest annual renewal, with Oceania the least, at about an order of magnitude less. Asia, with its large population, has the largest withdrawals, over five times more than the other regions of the world.

Table 2.2 Freshwater resources in different regions around the world

Region	Total volume liquid freshwater/ 1,000 km³	Annual freshwater renewals/ km³	Annual freshwater withdrawals/ km³	Freshwater withdrawals to renewals/ %
North America	2071	6812	602	8.8
South America	1299	12724	212	1.7
Europe	541	6572	277	4.2
Africa	2722	3931	259	6.6
Asia	3691	6071	2505	41.3
Oceania	324	902	26	2.9

Source: The United Nations World Water Development Report, 2022.

Note: Data are for 2017; one km³ is one billion m³.

Agriculture takes the lion's share of freshwater consumed in nearly all regions. In Asia and Africa, over 80% of the withdrawal is used to service this sector, with South America and Oceania not far behind. Water for industry accounts for between 40% and 50% in the most developed regions of North America and Europe; Africa, as the least developed region, uses just 9% for this purpose. Water for domestic use is less than 25% in all regions.

More than half of the world's population now resides in cities and will reach two-thirds by the middle of this century. This urbanisation brings with it growing water demand and shortages that will grow in the coming years and decades, especially in central Asia and the Middle East.

2.2.2   Groundwater resources

The UN estimates that approximately 99% of all liquid freshwater is groundwater, and its sustainable exploitation is critical for life on earth. Groundwater is water from rain or melting ice and snow that soaks into the soil and is stored in the pores between rocks and particles of soil. It is distributed over the entire world, but its abundance and the conditions for its access and recharge rates vary considerably.

Groundwater can stay underground for hundreds of thousands of years, or it can come to the surface and help fill rivers and streams, lakes, and wetlands. Groundwater can also come to the surface as a spring, or it can be pumped from a well. Groundwater can move through gravel and sandy deposits, and here an aquifer can form, which may be a few metres to thousands of kilometres thick and less than a square kilometre or hundreds of thousands of square kilometres in area.

Most groundwater is of good quality with natural contaminants such as iron. Contamination from the use of fertilisers, pesticides, industrial and mining wastes, and petroleum poses increasing threats to human health and the environment. Groundwater can be 'brackish' when it is slightly to moderately saline, with Total Dissolved Solids (TDS) – inorganic salts and small amounts of organic matter – concentrations in the range 1,600 mg per litre (or ppm) to 10,000 mg per litre. Brackish water can be used directly, or it can be treated to remove solids via desalination.

Table 2.3 summarises groundwater withdrawals by region and by sector. Over two-thirds of the world's groundwater withdrawals are in Asia, in part due to the large rural populations where it is the main source of freshwater. North America is the next largest at 16%, while the other regions are all well below 10% of the total extracted.

Agriculture takes the lion's share of the groundwater at almost 70% of the total; the domestic sector accounts for over 20%, with industry at just under 10% of the total. The distribution between the three main sectors differs markedly by region. For example, in Asia, the withdrawals amount to 76%, 16%, and 8% for agriculture, domestic, and industry, respectively; in Europe, the contributions for the three sectors are 36%, 45%, and 19%, respectively.

Table 2.3 Groundwater withdrawals by region and sector

Region	Groundwater withdrawal		Water use by sector /%		
	km³ per annum	*% of world*	*Agriculture*	*Domestic*	*Industry*
North America	156	16	62	30	7
South America	27	3	49	32	20
Europe	65	7	36	45	19
Africa	45	5	65	32	4
Asia	657	68	76	16	8
Australia and Oceania	8	1	48	48	3
World	959	100	69	22	9

Source: Groundwater. Making the Invisible Visible, The United Nations World Water Development Report, 2022.

Note: Data are for 2017; one km³ is one billion m³.

2.3 Water management options

There are various dimensions to the management of valuable freshwater resources, as shown in Table 2.4: supply-side and demand-side options and opportunities for the short-term and long-term. Also, there are those activities that require a reactive or proactive approach and those that are autonomous in nature or rely on government or business action. Also important is a recognition of the key stakeholders and their roles in each activity.

2.3.1 Supply-side measures

There are seven possible supply-side measures that can ease the pressure on freshwater resources. Three such measures can be deployed over the short term: rainwater harvesting, minimising leaks, water recycling and re-use, and groundwater development. The first is simply the collecting and storing of rainwater so that it can be re-used. This proactive measure is helpful to farmers and industry, and homeowners, supplementing their conventional water resources. An abstraction licence or planning permission is not required, nor is this activity regulated so long as there are no environmental issues.

Water leaks are a common occurrence, particularly in those countries that have old or poor infrastructure. Reducing leaks is a priority activity, benefiting both the supplier and the consumer, and it requires a commitment of resources by the water industry to maintain and improve the basic distribution infrastructure.

Groundwater and surface water are connected. Groundwater development increases water availability, playing a different role in normal and drought years; this can be a proactive measure, supplementing surface water under normal conditions, or a reactive measure by helping to mitigate the variable

Table 2.4 Managing water resources

	Short Term	Long Term
Supply side measures	• Rainwater harvesting • Minimising water leaks • Water Recycling and re-use • Groundwater development and use	• Storage and retention infrastructure • Groundwater development and use • Inter-basin transfer • Treatment and use of wastewater • Desalination
Demand side Measures	• Land use planning and management • River basin planning and management • Awareness raising and conservation	• Adoption of efficient water technologies and practices across all sectors • River basin planning and management • Awareness raising and conservation

Sources: Adapted from Water Futures and Solutions, Peter Burek et al., IIASA, 2016; Global Water Security, the Royal Academy of Engineering, 2011.

supply of water in drought conditions. Groundwater resources can be exploited autonomously by the farming and industry sectors and are overseen by, for example, government agencies such as basin authorities and by interested third parties such as environmental Non-Government Organisations (NGOs).

In terms of planned, longer-term measures, several large-scale developments are possible alongside groundwater exploitation, including water storage and retention infrastructure, treatment and use of wastewater, inter-basin transfer, and desalination. There are several natural water storage options, including aquifers, rivers, and wetlands, while man-made dams have also proved very effective. Enhancing or building new storage facilities can increase water supply for normal uses and address extreme conditions associated with climate change, for example, when there is too little water (droughts) or too much water (floods); in the case of dams, these facilities are also used to produce hydropower. The key stakeholders for this activity are government bodies, including the development, environment, and basin authorities, and industry; environmental NGOs also take a keen interest in these projects.

A further longer-term measure is the movement of water from water-rich to water-scarce regions. Once again, these large-scale man-made schemes are complex and require the participation of a range of stakeholders, from government agencies that can provide the planning and financing for such schemes to those sectors that would benefit.

Wastewater can be reused for different purposes once pollutants have been removed; the extent and nature of this cleansing are dependent on the use of the water. The water utilities play a key role here, as do other industries that make use of large volumes of water. Government regulators and environmental authorities play an important role in ensuring the quality of the water is fit-for-purpose.

2.3.2 *Demand-side measures*

There are three short-term demand-side measures that can relieve pressure on freshwater resources: land-use and river basin planning and management, and awareness raising initiatives. Land-use planning and management involves the promotion of water saving and the adoption of best practices such as crop residue management, conservation tillage to reduce soil erosion, irrigation metering and scheduling, water recycling in fields, and conversion to rainfed agriculture. Also important is a change in crop pattern and cropping intensity and the use of drought-tolerant crops. Key stakeholders here are the farmers and the agricultural experts that can support them; the government can provide incentives and development support.

Government and its authorities put limits on water extraction in the management of river basins. It provides efficient and fair allocation rules, clear property rights, and adjustment of operation rules; it also puts in place extreme event response. The implementation of these measures is to the benefit of all sectors – agriculture, industry, and domestic – that rely on river basins for freshwater.

The adoption of efficient technologies is an ongoing activity that has longer term benefits. This involves the deployment of efficient irrigation technologies (sprinkler and drip) and the retrofit of water devices in houses. The government and its agencies can play an important role here, not only by raising awareness about the importance of conserving water but also by providing incentives, such as appropriate water pricing, to encourage their adoption. Water in the domestic sector does not often discriminate between, for example, that which is used for drinking purposes and that which is used for washing purposes, and this may have to change in the future to optimise its treatment and use.

2.3.3 *Desalination*

The water industry, then, is working hard to meet the increasing demand for freshwater through improved management of water resources, water recycling, reuse, and harvesting, greater efficiency in use, and improvements in the water supply and distribution infrastructure. There has also been good progress in the development and deployment of desalination technology, the act of removing salt from saltwater or brackish water to produce pure water.

This technology has several positive attributes that make it an attractive option for many countries: the oceans provide a large resource of water, while 'brackish water', or water of a lower salt content found in estuaries, is also available as a feed resource. Desalination increases supply rather than constraining demand; it can be deployed widely, and there is significant potential for cost reduction in the future.

The estimated global fleet of about 16,000 plants operating in 2020 have a total capacity of about 95 million m^3 day or 35 km^3 per year. This amounts to over 3.5% of the global groundwater resource extraction of about

960 km^3 per year; the percentage contribution at the national level where this technology is deployed can be much higher.

As indicated in Chapter 1, the expectation is that the number of desalination plants around the world may double in the next 25 years. Plant size varies enormously depending on need, from a few tens of thousands to hundreds of thousands of cubic metres per day. The technology is deployed in most countries around the world, with the largest capacity in the Middle East (47%), East Asia and the Pacific (18%), North America (12%), and Western Europe (11%). Perhaps the most telling figure is that an estimated 300 million people around the world rely on desalinated water for some or all their daily needs. This number will rise significantly in the coming decades.

However, the technology also has some disadvantages, including the relatively high cost of production, in part because it is an energy-intensive activity, and, as demonstrated by the war in Ukraine, international energy prices can increase significantly. There are also two environmental impacts that need to be addressed: the discharge of brine into the marine environment local to the operating plants and carbon dioxide and, to a lesser extent, methane, emissions into the atmosphere.

Most of the plants operating today use fossil fuels to provide thermal and electrical energy, and, as indicated above, this brings with it economic and environmental costs. Increasingly, renewable technologies are being used to provide some of the electricity needs of new desalination plants.

An industry initiative, the Global Clean Water Alliance (H_2O minus CO_2), set clean energy targets for existing and new desalination plants in 2015. Existing water desalination plants, which were operational in 2015, should supply at least 10% of the annual energy demand from clean energy sources by 2030. New desalination plants commencing operation between 2020 and 2025 should supply at least 20% of the annual energy demand from clean energy sources; those commencing operation between 2026 and 2030 should supply at least 40%; those between 2031 and 2035 should supply at least 60%, and those plants commencing operation after 2035 should supply at least 80% of the annual energy demand.

The water industry, then, is working hard to reduce the environmental impact of desalination with a gradual shift to low-carbon electricity. Advances in technology are also expected to reduce the cost by up to 60% in the next 20 years. These developments will help make the technology more accessible to those countries that will be heavily impacted by climate change in the coming decades.

The ready availability of freshwater resources has been taken for granted in large parts of the world, but this will change in the future. There is ample evidence to suggest that traditional sources of freshwater are under pressure, and this pressure will increase further in the coming decades, driven by a growing global population, the associated economic activity, and more severe climate change impacts. Technology in the form of desalination will be essential for the water sector in some countries, as essential as renewable technologies are for electricity production in the longer term.

Desalinated water has many uses, for example, drinking water in Israel, mining in Chile, and ensuring the security of water supply in drought conditions in the south of the UK. There are several technologies, and these are discussed in Chapters 3 and 4, but one technology, Reverse Osmosis (RO), has emerged to dominate the sector. Here, a high-pressure saline water feed is passed through a membrane that prevents the salt ions from passing through, ultimately leading to two streams of water: pure water and a separate, more saline 'waste' mixture. Seawater or 'brackish' water can be used as feed water, and once through the membrane, the saline 'waste' is returned to its source, diluted by the sea or estuary from where it came.

2.3.4 *Water resources in selected countries*

The World Bank provides water databases for around 180 countries, and Table 2.5 summarises some of the key freshwater metrics for the selected country set in Table 2.1; also presented are global averages for comparison.

Table 2.5 Key freshwater metrics for selected countries

Continent	Country	Freshwater withdrawal as a proportion of available freshwater resources/ % [(1), (2)]	Annual freshwater withdrawals/ Billion cubic meters [(3)]	Annual freshwater withdrawals/ % of internal resources [(3)]	Renewable water resources/ cubic meters per capita [(2)]	Price of tap water in selected cities and countries/ $ per 500 mL [(4)]
Middle East	Saudi Arabia	1000	21.2	883	71	0.04
	Israel	96	1.2	160	84	3.3
North Africa	Morocco	51	10.6	37	805	1.2
Europe	Spain	43	31.2	28	2376	2.2
	Cyprus	28	0.2	28	656	n/a
	UK	14	8.4	6	2182	3.5
North America	USA	28	444.4	16	8622	2.8
South America	Chile	22	35.4	4	47253	1.2
Asia	China	43 [(5)]	591.8	21	2005	0.6
Oceania	Australia	5	15.9	3	19694	4.2
Global Average		70 [(6)]	n/a	119 [(7)]	14946 [(8)]	2.3 [(9)]

Sources: World Development Indicators, The World Bank, 2022; The Water Price Index, www.holidu.com., 2022.

Notes: (1), Water stress; (2), Data are for 2018; (3), Data are for 2017; (4), Data are for 2021; (5), value is for 2017; (6), Average of 176 States; (7), Average of 182 States; (8), Average of 185 States; (9), Average of 120 cities in 63 countries; n/a is not available.

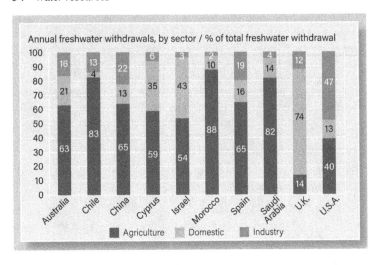

Figure 2.6 Water use in selected countries

Source: World Development Indicators, The World Bank, 2022.

An important metric is the freshwater withdrawal as a proportion of internal resources, and the UN suggests that water scarcity occurs when this value exceeds 25%. Five of the countries in the case study set currently exceeded this value, with Saudi Arabia and Israel, particularly water stressed, at about 880% and 160%, respectively, in 2017. It is not surprising that desalination, using readily accessible seawater, is an important source of pure water in these countries.

Interestingly, the UK and Chile are well below the UN's benchmark, but parts of these countries suffer from freshwater shortages. The UK is a well-developed country, while Chile is less so, yet both require better infrastructure to transport freshwater from water-rich regions to those less well-endowed with this commodity. To address shortages, both countries have desalination plants, although the water produced is used for very different purposes: the UK as a contingency measure and Chile for the mining industry. Two countries – Spain and Cyprus – are on the margin of the UN's benchmark, reflecting the fact that they suffer from periods of drought; Cyprus is recognised as being the most water scarce country in Europe.

The price of tap water in the cities of the selected countries varies significantly. The lowest is in Saudi Arabia, where water is heavily subsidised, while at the higher end, consumers in Israel, the UK, and Australia pay between eight and ten times more for their water.

Summary key points

- Available surface water resources at continent level remain relatively constant, but many countries are experiencing water scarcity conditions.
- Freshwater consumption has increased by a factor of six over the last 100 years and is likely to rise by a further 35% in the period to 2050. The drivers for this increase include social, economic, and environmental factors.
- Population growth and migration from rural to urban centres have increased demand for freshwater, as have economic development and food production. Climate change has exacerbated the issue of changing weather patterns, from an increase in extreme weather events to more prevalent drought conditions and aridification.
- There are major regional differences in both the availability and consumption of freshwater resources. Asia, with its large population, consumes over 40% of the total, with the other regions around the world each consuming less than 10%.
- Almost all countries in a belt around 10°–40° North, from Mexico to China, including Southern Europe, are currently affected by water scarcity, together with parts of Australia, Western South America, and Southern Africa.
- Agriculture and food production take the lion's share of the water consumed, with a global average of almost 70% of the total; the domestic sector is the next largest at over 20%, with industry accounting for less than 10% of the total. There are significant regional and country-level differences, with those that are more developed tending to use more water for domestic and industry sectors.
- Desalination has several attributes that make it an attractive option for the provision of potable water. It makes a small but growing contribution to global freshwater supplies, and it makes a very significant contribution in some countries, without which life would be very difficult.

3   Desalination today

Desalination is to the water industry as renewables are to the energy sector.

3.1   Context for the industry

The nature and scale of the role desalination plays in a country or region are determined by several factors: the availability or otherwise of freshwater, the key drivers for water demand such as population growth, social and economic development, and the impacts of climate change. Like all infrastructure, desalination involves a range of stakeholders, and the successful deployment of the technology relies on addressing their concerns and meeting their needs.

3.1.1   Dimensions of desalination

There are many dimensions of desalination, broadly classified into two areas: those that are related to its deployment and those that are related to the industry, as shown in Table 3.1. They begin with the need for pure water: at one end of the spectrum, it may be essential for human and animal welfare, or at the other end, it provides valuable contingency resources in times of drought conditions. The way in which the water is used is another important dimension: it is mainly used for drinking purposes but can also be used for irrigation purposes and industrial use.

As with all technologies, there are environmental impacts associated with the process waste streams, from air pollution to potential damage to marine ecosystems. There are also a range of stakeholders involved that determine the ambition and success of the industry; for example, the government provides the policy, regulations, and incentives so that industry can deploy, operate, and maintain the facilities, while communities where plants are operating or where new plants are planned are also increasingly vocal.

The maturity of the industry in a jurisdiction is an important issue for deployment, with the industry and its supply chain well developed in some countries and new to others. The requirement may be for small-scale plants,

DOI: 10.4324/9781003334224-3

Table 3.1 Dimensions of desalination

Themes		Aspects		
Desalination deployment	Role	Essential to human life	Contingency use	
	Climate drivers	Drought conditions	Extreme events	
	Sector served	Domestic	Agriculture and industry	
	Environment	Air pollution	Marine ecosystems	
	Stakeholders	Industry	Local communities	
Desalination industry	Maturity	Well established	New to the country	
	Scale	Small scale	Large scale	
	Feedwater	Seawater	Brackish water	
	Technology	Thermal	Mechanical	
	Price of water	Absolute	Relative to alternatives	

Source: Author's assessment.

or, as occurs in some countries, only large-scale deployment can meet the needs of the population. Geography and hydrology play an important role, particularly in the feedwater resources available to the desalination sector. Some countries may deploy the technology close to the coast for ready access to seawater, while others may deploy it in areas where brackish water is used as the feedwater resource.

The technologies deployed to desalinate water can, in the main, be classified into those that use a thermal process and those that use mechanical means such as filtration. The cost of production and the price charged to consumers, both in absolute terms and relative to other freshwater sources, are also key issues.

Each country will have its own unique characteristics touching different dimensions. This is explored more fully in the country case studies presented in Chapter 5.

3.1.2 Key stakeholders

There are three main groups of stakeholders, outlined in Table 3.2, the first of which are those with a strong interest in the water industry and its practices. This group includes the public who want access to plentiful supplies of clean drinking water at a reasonable price; it also includes interest groups and Non-Governmental Organisations (NGOs) who campaign on behalf of those who do not have such access but are also very keen to protect the local environment from potentially damaging waste streams.

The institutions, both academic and professional, play an important role in pushing the technological envelope of the industry through innovation, establishing standards for the industry to adhere to, and providing skills development programmes. Also important in this group is the media, who have a role in scrutinising industry practices for the public, as they do in many other areas.

Table 3.2 Stakeholder interests

Stakeholder groups	Key stakeholders	Stakeholder interest
Those with an interest in the water industry and its practices	Public	Want secure and clean water supplies
	Institutions	Provide technological innovation, standards, and education and skills development
	Interest Groups	Demand action on behalf of those that lack clean water and on environmental protection
	Media	Provide scrutiny and transparency for public interest
Those who create the environment for the industry	Government	Encourage investment in national water infrastructure
	Officials and Regulators	Ensure provision of clean supplies of water and protection of the environment
	Local Politicians	Protect and promote the interests of the local communities
	Government Opposition	Scrutinise Government policies and highlight failings
Those who have direct interests in the industry	Market Participants	Deliver and operate water infrastructure
	Investors	Invest in water infrastructure projects
	Employees	Want high-skilled and well-rewarded jobs
	Local Communities	Want jobs and protection of the local environment

Source: Author's assessment.

The second group involves those who create the environment for the industry to flourish. Key amongst these is the government, as custodians of the well-being of its citizens; they must ensure the security of supply of water for its population and that the industry has access to energy, which is a very important enabler for desalination. These require policies, regulation, and incentives to help bring forward and maintain new plants in both the water and energy sectors, mostly separately but increasingly working together on the same site. The government, then, is a key facilitator, with the Minister responsible for the water industry giving a clear policy signal that it wishes to see the deployment of desalination technology; it also needs to provide the right incentives for the industry to invest in and operate new facilities.

Other politicians also have a role to play by providing valuable scrutiny and comment on the minister's policies, leading to better overall decision-making for the country. Local politicians are also important since their main concern is the well-being of their local communities, where the desalination plants are located. They must balance the economic benefits that such facilities bring to the community with the potential environmental impact associated with the building and operation of the plant.

Government officials have the responsibility for implementing policy decisions and ensuring that desalinated production is integrated into the wider water industry. Water and energy regulators must not only ensure that water standards are always met but must also make sure the environment is protected from the waste streams produced by water and energy plants.

The third stakeholder group includes those that have direct interests in the running of the water industry and, within that, the desalination sector. The water industry and its investors are tasked with maintaining the security of water supply by building and operating the basic infrastructure and at a price the consumer can afford. They are supported by a global supply chain which has emerged over the last few decades, one that can service the needs of a growing desalination sector and bring forward innovations to improve plant performance. The energy industry is also a key enabler for desalination, and developments in this sector, such as the drive for greater renewables deployment, have a major impact on the water sector.

Employees are also an important part of this group, with overall responsibility for the site. They need to be expert in operating the plant, to maintain its integrity, and, as a minimum, to comply with safety protocols and environmental law as it applies to plant activities in their jurisdiction. Their employment brings much-needed economic benefit to the communities in which they operate.

Local communities often welcome investment and highly skilled jobs into their area, but they also engage with industry to ensure that sensitive environments are protected. Local activists are not only committed to their cause but also skilled at lobbying decision-makers in government and influential third parties. Such activists, often supported by mainstream NGOs, have stopped the development of new desalination plants in recent years in, for example, the UK and Australia. It is inevitable that some of the many plants the industry wants to build in the coming decades will not go ahead because of local opposition.

3.2   Current status of the desalination industry

The desalination sector has grown significantly over the last 60 years. The number of desalination plants in 1960 was under 100; 20 years later, this number had increased to about 2,000, and by the turn of the century, the number was over 9,000. In 2020, the *cumulative* number of plants built was close to 20,000, but some of these were no longer working, and the number in operation is estimated at about 16,000 plants worldwide.

As the number of plants has grown, so has the total water production capacity. In 1960, the total production by the 100 or so plants was just 0.1 million cubic metres (m^3) per day; by 2020, the total production capacity

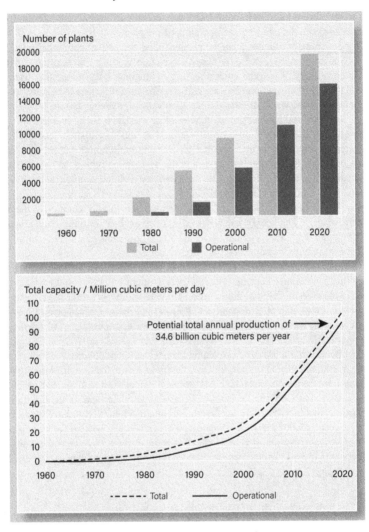

Figure 3.1 Global deployment of desalination technology

Source: Adapted from The state of desalination and brine production: A global outlook, Edward Jones et al., Science of the Total Environment, Volume 657, p1343, 2019.

by operational plants had increased to about 95 million m³ per day, or 35 billion m³ per year. This is the nameplate production capacity, or the maximum design specification for the global operational fleet, but not all the plants will be working to their optimum value all the time.

The average production capacity per plant has also grown steadily over this period, from 1,200 m³ per day to 5,200 m³ per day. However, the latter disguises the huge progress made by the industry in increasing the size of plant to meet the growing demand for pure water in some water-stressed countries. For example, the largest plant site today is in Saudi Arabia, which has a production capacity of just over 1 million m³ per day. Indeed, the Middle East is host to the ten largest plants in the world, with four in Saudi Arabia, three in the UAE, two in Israel, and one in Dubai. The smallest of the ten plants, in Israel, has a capacity of 570,000 m³ per day, over two orders of magnitude bigger than the average plant deployed in 2020. The size of the plant deployed will depend on several factors, starting with the nature of the feedwater available and the scale of the need for pure water, but there is an expectation that the *average* capacity of the global fleet will continue to rise over the next 30 years or so.

3.2.1 Regional distribution of desalination plant

There are 193 member countries of the UN and remarkably 177 of these, or over 90% of the total, are reported to have desalination facilities, each with its own needs in terms of size and purpose. The Middle East and North Africa countries account for about 4,800, or 30% of the 16,000 operational plants; these plants account for almost 48% of the global production capacity of 95 million m³ per day. This is perhaps not surprising because, as indicated above, the ten largest plants in the world are in this region and together account for over 7 million m³ per day of the region's 45 million m³ per day. The average plant size of its desalination fleet is just under 9400 m³ per day; this is considerably larger than the average in all other regions, even if the ten largest plants are excluded from the analysis.

The next largest region in terms of number of plants is East Asia and the Pacific which has about 3,500 plants, a total daily production capacity of about 17.5 million m³ per day, and an average daily production capacity of 5,000 m³ per day. North America and Western Europe are third and fourth in terms of number of plants. The former has about 2,340 operating plants with an average plant capacity of almost 5,000 m³ per day, delivering a total production of just over 11 million m³ per day; Western Europe also has about 2,340 operating plants but with a lower average plant capacity of about 3,750 m³ per day, delivering a total production of almost 9 million m³ per day.

The remaining four regions – Latin America and Caribbean, Southern Asia, Eastern Europe and Central Asia, and Sub-Saharan Africa – together have about 2,900 plants located in their countries, or just over 18% of the total

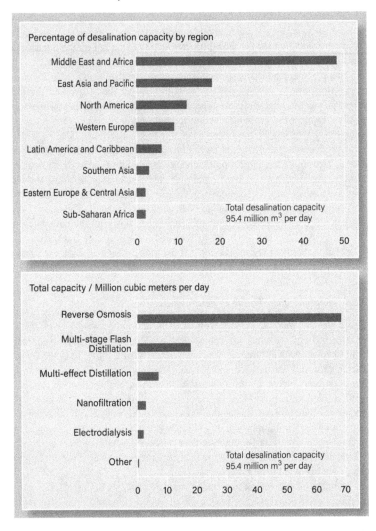

Figure 3.2 Deployment of desalination by region and technology

Source: Adapted from The state of desalination and brine production: A global outlook, Edward Jones et al., Science of the Total Environment, Volume 657, p1343, 2019.

operational plants, with a combined daily production capacity of over 12 million m³ per day. The average daily plant capacity across these four regions is about 4,300 m³ per day, less than half that of the Middle East and North Africa region.

Desalination is an expensive technology to operate, and this, in part, is reflected in the geographical deployment of plants. Two-thirds of plants are in those countries with high-income levels, and just under a third are in middle-income countries; less than 50 plants, or 0.3% of the global fleet, have been built in low-income countries, even though it is often in these countries where the need for water is greatest. It is important that innovation and scale are used to deliver a reduction in the cost of water if those countries suffering from water scarcity and with low incomes are to benefit from this technology.

Three sectors use the production of desalinated water: domestic or municipal for drinking water, industry including power generation, and agriculture. At the global level, over 60% of the total daily desalination production of 95 million m³ per day is used for municipal purposes, with the industrial sector accounting for a further 35%; irrigation accounts for less than 2% of the total production. These values differ by region and by country.

3.3 Desalination technologies

The past 150 years has seen many technologies emerge and compete to satisfy a particular need in energy, transport, and communications. In the water industry, that need is an increasing demand for freshwater in many parts of the world. What is also interesting is that across industries and over time the 'winning' technologies emerge because they perform best in terms of cost, or have superior technical and environmental performance, or a combination of the two. The role of innovation, then, is crucial in improving technical performance, making it easier to deploy and operate in existing and new jurisdictions.

In very simple terms, desalination is a chemical process with a feedstock, a process, a product, and a waste. The feedstock is water that has relatively large amounts of dissolved solids (salts), such as seawater or brackish water. The process involves the separation of salt from the saline water, yielding a salt-free, pure water product which can replace or supplement natural freshwater supplies. There is also waste in the form of a saline-enriched residue, or brine, that is sent back into the reservoir where it came from to be heavily diluted and, by doing so minimise damage to the local marine environment.

As with all chemical processes, energy is required in significant quantities, and unless it is indigenous to the country, this energy can be expensive. Gaseous emissions from its use have environmental implications at the regional level (sulphur and nitrogen oxides) and global level (carbon dioxide).

The former can be minimised by using the appropriate abatement technology that is now commonly available; unfortunately, carbon dioxide capture and storage has still to be developed on a commercial scale, so this greenhouse gas is vented into the atmosphere.

There are at least 16 technologies to desalinate water, some mature and in the mainstream of the industry, others in development; they can be used on their own or in combinations to increase process efficiency and freshwater quality. They can be grouped by working principle: evaporation and condensation, filtration, and crystallisation. They may also be grouped by the energy used since this plays a critical part in the process: thermal, mechanical, electrical, and chemical. The energy used and the associated environmental implications are discussed in Chapter 4.

3.3.1   Commercial mainstream desalination technologies

There are six commercial technologies deployed for widespread application, one group based on the use of an evaporation and condensation process, while a second group uses membranes. The former, in very simple terms, uses heat to turn water into steam; the steam, which contains no salt, is cooled and turned back into liquid water, leaving the salt behind in a concentrated saline solution or brine. Vapour compression distillation is a process for producing water with relatively low energy consumption, and compression can be carried out with a mechanical or thermal process. In the membrane group, high pressure is used to force water through a membrane that is impermeable to salt; the salt is trapped and disposed of in a more concentrated saline or brine solution residue.

Distillation processes

There are four distillation processes: Multi-Stage Flash (MSF) distillation, Multi-Effect Distillation (MED), Mechanical Vapour Compression (MVC) and Thermal Vapour Compression (TVC); apart from the TVC process, these technologies are used in large scale application.

1) In the MSF process feedwater and seawater, for example, is heated from ambient temperature to 85°C at atmospheric pressure, just over 1,000 millibar (mbar) at ground level. It then passes into a series of chambers where the pressure, set at about 60 mbar, is lower than the saturation pressure. The water is superheated and boils spontaneously, returning to the thermodynamic equilibrium state of 60 mbar and 35°C. The steam produced is condensed using seawater to produce pure (or potable) water, and this has the additional benefit of contributing to preheating the feedwater for the process.

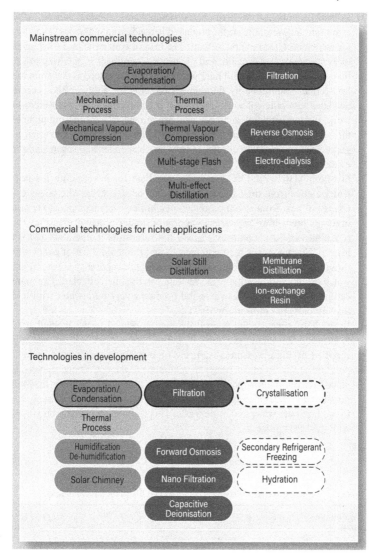

Figure 3.3 Desalination sector rich in technologies

Source: Based on A Review of Water Desalination Technologies, Curto et al., Applied Sciences, Volume 11, p670, 2021.

2) In the MED process, thermal energy is supplied to the first evaporator to evaporate seawater; the steam produced is condensed in the next evaporator, which is called the first 'effect'. The heat of condensation is then used to evaporate seawater again, and the process continues in this way to the final condenser. The overall pure water flow rate produced is that from the first 'effect' multiplied by the number of 'effects', although the process becomes less efficient as it progresses to completion. For the system to work, the temperatures and pressures are graded in a decreasing manner through the process, from the head evaporator to the final condenser, to guarantee a temperature difference between the condensing steam, and the evaporating seawater.

3) For both MVC and TVC processes, the heat for evaporating the seawater comes from the compression of vapour rather than the direct exchange of heat from steam produced in a boiler. The mechanical version involves preheating seawater evaporation under reduced pressure; the resulting vapour is compressed, and the saturation temperature is then higher. This vapour is then condensed, and the latent heat of condensation is used in the evaporator-condenser unit to evaporate seawater. Pure water and the more saline brine residue can then be collected. The plant can treat brackish and seawater and produces very pure water with less than 10 parts per million (ppm) TDS.

4) In the TVC process, the main difference is related to the method used to increase the vapour pressure. A thermal compressor is used which is supplied by high pressure steam; the high-pressure steam pulls in low-pressure steam to make steam at medium-pressure. Compression takes place between the low-pressure steam taken in, and the resultant medium pressure mixture. Once again, the latent heat is used to evaporate seawater to produce pure water and brine waste. This technology is commonly used with the MED process.

Table 3.3 Some basic characteristics of mainstream distillation technologies

Characteristic	MSF	MED	MCV	MED-TVC
Head temperature °C	<120	<70	<70	<70
Main energy source	Steam	Steam, hot water	Electricity	Steam
Heat consumption in kWh per m³	70–80	50–70	0	50–60
Electrical consumption kWh per m³	3.5	1.5	8–14	1.5

Source: Desalination of Seawater and Brackish water, Philippe Bandelier, www. Encyclopedie-Energie.Org, 2021.

Membrane processes

There are two commercial membrane technologies: Reverse Osmosis (RO) and Electrodialysis (ED), the former is deployed on a large scale, while the latter is used for small-scale applications.

1) Osmosis occurs naturally where a dilute solution is transported across a semi-permeable membrane towards a more concentrated solution on the other side; RO, as the name implies, is the opposite. In osmosis, the solvent water passes through the membrane until the pressure difference across the membrane, about 350 pounds per square inch or 25 kg force per square cm for a fresh water-seawater interface, is equal to the osmotic pressure.

   Reverse Osmosis, then, occurs when a pressure greater than the osmotic pressure is applied to the saline water, causing freshwater to flow through the membrane while holding back dissolved solids (salts). The higher the applied pressure above the osmotic pressure, the higher the rate of freshwater that flows across the membranes.

   The technology has a relatively low capital cost, is easily scaled to match demand, and uses electricity to apply pressure. However, there are limitations, such as relatively low water quality when compared to the distillation processes.

2) Salt in water takes the form of ions, which move under the influence of an electric field. ED uses an electrical field and membranes that are permeable to same-charge ions but relatively impermeable to opposite-charge ions to remove ionised materials from feedwater.

   Although relatively energy intensive when compared to RO, for example, ED requires less feedwater pre-treatment than pressure-driven membrane processes. It also delivers high-purity water, and the energy consumption used is dependent on the salinity of the feedwater and the quality of water desired. However, the technology is only appropriate for brackish water.

3.3.2 Commercial technologies for specialist applications

There are currently three commercial technologies used for specific, small-scale niche applications: membrane distillation is used in food production, ion exchange resin is used to produce demineralised water, and solar still distillation is appropriate for other small-scale applications.

1) Membrane distillation is a separation technology which has a membrane filter between a cold solution on one side and a hot solution on the other side. It does not need pressure and benefits from low operating temperatures.

2) Ion exchange resin involves removing certain contaminants from water by essentially exchanging the contaminant with an ionic substance that is considerably safer for humans. It can only be used with feedwater of low salinity, such as brackish water.

3) Solar still distillation uses, as the name implies, solar energy to warm up and cause evaporation from saltwater or brackish water; the evaporated water is condensed within the same closed system. The still can be constructed with ordinary materials but can only be used for small applications.

3.3.3   Desalination technologies under development

There are at least seven technologies in development: two based on thermal principles, three that utilise membrane technology, and a further two technologies that use crystallisation as a method of separation.

1) The Humidification-Dehumidification and Solar Chimney technologies are very simple in concept. The former comprises a humidifier, a dehumidifier, and a heater for low-temperature operation. Air is humidified through direct contact with saline water in a humidifier; the hot, moist air is put in indirect contact with cold saline water in a dehumidifier, which causes water vapour to condense, producing desalinated water. Although simple, it can be a challenge to get the various flow streams optimised.

2) In the Solar Chimney technology, the air enters a solar (thermal) collector, gets heated, and then enters the bottom of a 'chimney'. The air rises and becomes humid by spraying saline water into the rising hot air stream, causing evaporation followed by condensation to give desalinated water. This technology has good potential, particularly in regions rich in solar energy.

3) Forward Osmosis is the passage of water through a semi-permeable membrane due to an osmotic pressure gradient, leaving a solution with a higher level of contaminants on one side of the membrane. The technology has the advantage of consuming low thermal energy and can be used to treat, for example, wastewater to extract pure water from an effluent stream, leaving a more concentrated waste product.

4) Nanofiltration is also a membrane filtration technology in which pressure is applied to a liquid stream, driving it through a semi-permeable membrane to remove dissolved solids. This is a relatively low-energy process that produces a dilute saline solution.

5) Capacitive De-Ionisation technology removes salt ions from water by applying an electrical voltage difference between two porous carbon electrodes in which the ions are temporarily stored. This is a relatively efficient process, but it can only accommodate water with low contaminants, as occurs in brackish water resources.

6) Secondary Refrigerant Freezing saltwater creates ice crystals that are essentially made up of pure water. There are three steps involved: ice formation, ice cleaning, and ice melting. This technology has good commercial potential going forward because of its efficiency, but ice removal can be a problem.

7) In Hydration technology, water is recovered in the form of gas or 'cage-like' hydrate crystals. Any dissolved ions and salts are excluded from the hydrate crystals during hydrate formation due to the size of the hydrate 'cages'. As with some of the new technologies, it benefits from relatively high efficiency but is expensive.

3.3.4 Supporting infrastructure needed for the desalination process

There is significant infrastructure in and around the desalination site. Large intake pipes are needed to ensure reliable access to feedwater sources such as the sea, rivers and their estuaries, aquifers, or wastewater; similar-sized outfall pipes return the brine residue waste back to the original source. Their location, then, will be dependent on the local conditions, and in particular, their ability to dilute the residue to levels that minimise the impact on marine and other ecosystems. This is a particular concern for local stakeholders and environmental groups, and detailed Environmental Impact Assessments (EIAs) are carried out before development is approved; ongoing monitoring of the local environment will also be required as part of the plant's licence-to-operate.

Facilities have intake screens that separate unwanted solids from the feedwater before entering the pre-treatment stage; this is particularly important when seawater resources are used. It is an essential step for RO plant, and although it will not remove all impurities, this helps improve the overall performance of the plant by reducing pressure on the desalination process; it uses less energy, lowers operation and maintenance costs, and lengthens the lifespan of the membrane.

Product water from desalination processes can be low in mineral content, hardness, alkalinity, and pH, and requires post-treatment to prepare it for human consumption. Water from MSF desalination units is remineralised by adding hydrated lime and CO_2, chlorinated by the injection of chlorine gas, and aerated with compressed air. These remineralisation steps result in, for example, raising pH, alkalinity, and hardness of the water, thereby 'stabilising' the water. Table 3.4 is an example of the kinds of post-treatment options for different combinations of feedwater sources and membrane technologies.

The final stage in the overall process is the storage of the water in tanks or ponds, ready for use when needed. The physical, chemical, and biological characteristics of water are continuously monitored at the site to ensure it is of the right quality, and the data made available for scrutiny by the appropriate authority.

Table 3.4 Illustration of potential post-treatment actions

Feedwater	Technology	Potential post-treatment actions
Seawater	Reverse Osmosis	• Re-carbonation • Lime addition • Calcite bed filtration • pH and/or alkalinity adjustment • Addition of corrosion inhibitors • Primary and secondary disinfection • Blending with fresh water supplies.
Brackish water (surface)	Reverse Osmosis Nanofiltration Electrodialysis	• pH and/or alkalinity adjustment • Addition of corrosion inhibitors • Primary and secondary disinfection • Blending with fresh water supplies
Brackish water (ground)	Reverse Osmosis Nanofiltration Electrodialysis	• Decarbonation (degasification) • Hydrogen sulphide stripping • pH and/or alkalinity adjustment • Addition of corrosion inhibitors • Primary and secondary disinfection • Blending with fresh water supplies • Bypass blending with raw water supply

Source: Desalination Post-Treatment Considerations, Steven J. Duranceau, Florida Water Resources Journal, November 2009.

3.4   The 'winning' desalination technologies

As indicated above, there are many technologies that have been used or are under development to desalinate water, and as with other technological revolutions, the 'winning' technologies have emerged from the pack. Cost decline plays an important role in this competition, but there are other factors: innovation potential, scalability, the type of feedwater available, whether indigenous energy resources are available or imported, and the overall environmental impact of the technology. RO is the 'winning' technology, but the thermal technologies of MSF and MED continue to play an important role in some countries.

3.4.1   *Assessment by technology*

Over 84% of the 16,000 operational plants in the world use RO technology, with MSF and MED accounting for just over 2% and just under 6% of the total, respectively; ED technology has also been deployed in significant numbers, accounting for just under 6% of the total. However, their contribution to global production capacity is somewhat different, with RO accounting for 69% of the total, MSF 18%, and MED 7%; the remaining technologies together account for less than 6% of total production capacity.

Of the ten largest operating plants, all in the Middle East where energy supplies are plentiful and cheap, six are purely RO, one is MSF, one is MED,

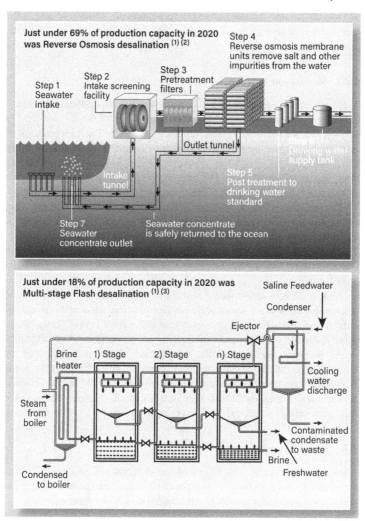

Figure 3.4 Main desalination technologies

Sources: (1), The state of desalination and brine production: A global outlook, Edward Jones et al., Science of the Total Environment, Volume 657, p1343, 2019; (2), Cities turn to desalination for water security, but at what cost? www.theconversation.com, February 11, 2019; (3), A Review of Water Desalination Technologies, Curto et al., Applied Sciences, Volume 11, p670, 2021.

and two sites utilise both RO and MSF technology; this perhaps explains the fact that despite only having 2% of the plants, MSF plants deliver 18% of the global production capacity.

3.4.2   Assessment by feedwater

There are several sources of feedwater, each with its own distinctive qualities – in the form of inorganic materials (salts) dissolved in the water – and this has implications for the desalination technology adopted. The concentration of salts in water is usually expressed in ppm of Total Dissolved Solids (TDS). The World Health Organisation recommends that drinking water contain no more than 500 ppm of TDS. The best high-quality municipal water can be as low as 50 ppm. Water for industrial purposes may need to be even lower.

As indicated earlier, feedwater for desalination plants may be seawater, brackish water, or other water resources, such as river water and wastewater, that cannot be used directly without treatment because of its quality. The concentration of salts in seawater varies from 20,000 to 55,000 ppm and sometimes even higher; brackish waters usually fall between 1,500 and 20,000 ppm.

Almost 38% of desalination plants draw on brackish water resources, whereas about 34% use seawater. Plants that use river water and low-salinity water to source desalination plants each account for about 11% of plants. Wastewater is also recycled via desalination plants and accounts for 6% of all plants.

As with the technologies, the contribution to production capacity by feedwater type is different to the number of plants involved. For example, plants that use seawater have 61% of the total production capacity, while that for brackish water amounts to just 21%; the production capacity of plants that use river water, low-salinity water, and wastewater together amounts to 18% of the total.

3.5   Some key issues

There is an expectation that the desalination sector will grow significantly over the next few decades as a burgeoning population and climate change put pressure on freshwater resources. The desalination sector must be able to address several challenges if it is to meet expectations. Many of these challenges are captured by a project risk matrix for this technology, and beyond that, by the ability of the industry and its supply chain to continue innovating.

3.5.1   Project risk matrix

All infrastructure projects have risks associated with them. They can be grouped into high, medium, and low risk and individual risks within each of these groups must be addressed for a successful project. Many infrastructure projects involve public-private partnerships, and it is important

Table 3.5 Establishing key project risks

	Minor	IMPACT	Major
High	Environmental Risk	Operation Risk	Project Management Risk
PROBABILITY	Legal Risk	Regulatory Risk	Construction Risk
	Reputational risk	Political Risk	Technology Risk
Low	Ethical Risk	Social Risk	Market Risk

Source: *Private Communication*, Olivier Carret, 2021.

that there is an understanding as to where the risks are allocated so that they can be successfully mitigated.

Risks can be mapped on two axes, one that indicates the potential *impact* of an issue or activity, and a second is an assessment of the *probability* of that risk being realised, and these are shown in Table 3.5. Clearly, the highest risk activities are those that have high-impact and high-probability outcomes, while the lowest risk activities are those that have a low-impact and low-probability outcome. For example, plant construction is a high-risk activity because any delay in commissioning the plant has significant financial implications by incurring additional costs, a loss of revenue, and potential penalties for not being able to fulfil contracts for the water produced; this is also the case if a plant is not returned to service on time and budget following an outage, planned or unplanned.

An example of a low-risk activity is likely to be the social risk associated with the project because there is an assumption that the project would have had to consult extensively with a range of stakeholders as part of the project development phase. A positive response would be needed, particularly from local communities, before the project would proceed to the capital-intensive construction phase.

Managing key risks

There are several areas of activity that need to be addressed for the successful deployment and operation of a desalination plant: choice of technology, secure energy supplies, contracts for freshwater produced, and measures to protect the local environment. There are several contributions to the cost of desalination: direct capital costs (30–40% of the total cost), power costs (20–35%), indirect capital costs (10–20%) and other operational and maintenance costs (15–30%). The overall project risk is reduced if each of these is managed efficiently.

As indicated above, the 'winning' technologies for mainstream use have emerged in the form of RO, MSF, and to a lesser extent, MED. The choice of technology relies on, for example, the scale of operation needed, a good technical understanding of the technology involved, the nature of the feedwater, the ready availability of energy supplies, and the overall cost per unit of freshwater.

In terms of scalability, RO plants are easily deployed across a reasonable capacity range, although not yet on the scale of MSF; this and the fact that the technology is relatively straightforward to operate and has high recovery ratios across all types of feedwaters help explain why it is the most popular technology option today. There are, however, potential risks to be mitigated, such as the quality of membranes, which can affect both production efficiency and energy consumption.

The deployment and operation of desalination plants relies on a good working relationship between those in government, both national and local, and those in industry. In particular, there needs to be confidence among those investing in the building and operation of the plants that the necessary contracts for desalinated water are forthcoming and for an extended period. The nature, scale, and longevity of the contract will depend on several factors, including the indigenous freshwater resources available, the propensity for drought conditions, the potential demand for water today and in the future, the effectiveness of water conservation measures, and, in extreme situations, the possibility of rationing.

All desalination technologies are energy intensive, be it in the form of thermal energy or electricity, and some are more energy intensive than others. In any event, the plants cannot operate without energy, and there are two options: secure the energy through the energy market as needed or, more likely, sign longer-term supply contracts. The latter is the preferred option and mitigates the risk of not having the energy when needed to fulfil water production contracts. It also means a major production cost can be better reflected in the water contracts.

It is a requirement that operators comply with the law in terms of environmental protection. The risks associated with this aspect of the project can be mitigated by carrying out a thorough environmental assessment and securing the necessary environmental permits and approvals secured; the latter will draw on the information available from other similar plants and environments.

Transparency is critical to engendering trust among stakeholders. It is incumbent, then, on the operator to monitor their emissions and provide regular reports to the authorities and local communities of any potential impact of their emissions on the local environment. Over time, it is possible that there is evidence of damage associated with plant operation, and remedial action will be needed to minimise that damage and allow the local environment to recover.

3.5.2   *Price of water and its relationship to quality*

The price of water varies significantly across the world and depends on a variety of factors, including, for example, the nature, scale, and quality of available renewable water resources, the water treatment and delivery infrastructure, and the quality of the water provided. There is also a difference in price between tap water and bottled water.

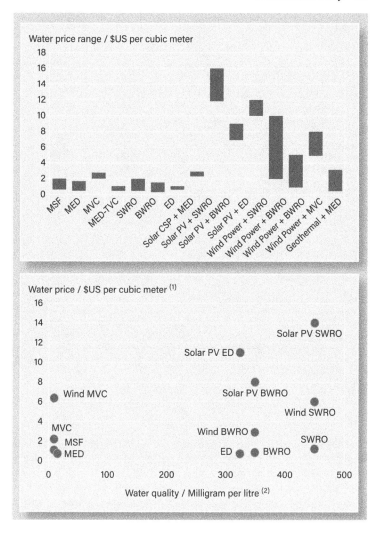

Figure 3.5 Price and quality of water by desalination technology

Source: Desalination of Seawater and Brackish water, P Bandelier, www.Encyclopedie-Energie.
Org, 2021.

Notes: (1), All numbers are averages; (2), 1 milligram of salt in water = I part per million. MSF,
Multi-Stage Flash; MED, Multi-Effect Distillation; MVC, Mechanical Vapour Condensation;
TVC, Thermal Vapour Condensation; SWRO, Seawater Reverse Osmosis; BWRO, Brackish Water
Reverse Osmosis; Electrodialysis; CSP, Concentrated Solar Power; PV, Photo-Voltaic.

Table 3.6 Economics of desalination technologies

Technology	Water quality/ ppm	Investment US$/(m³/day)	Water price/ (US$/m³)
Multi-Stage Flash Distillation	10	1850	1.3
Multi-Effect Distillation	10	1450	1.0
Mechanical Vapour Compression	10	2300	2.3
Mechanical Vapour Compression – Thermal Vapour Compression	10	1500	0.8
Seawater – Reverse Osmosis	450	1700	1.3
Brackish Water – Reverse Osmosis	350	750	0.9
Electrodialysis	325	350	0.8
Concentrated Solar Power – Multi-Effect Distillation	10	1450	2.6
Solar Photovoltaic – Seawater Reverse Osmosis	450	1700	14.0
Solar Photovoltaic – Brackish Water Reverse Osmosis	350	750	8.0
Solar Photovoltaic – Electrodialysis	325	350	11.0
Wind Power – Seawater Reverse Osmosis	450	1700	6.0
Wind – Power Brackish Water Reverse Osmosis	350	750	3.0
Wind Power – Mechanical Vapour Compression	10	2300	6.5
Geothermal – Multi-Effect Distillation	10	1450	2.5

Source: Desalination of Seawater and Brackish water, Philippe Bandelier, www. Encyclopedie-Energie.Org, 2021.

Note: All numbers are averages; I part per million is 1 milligram of salt in water.

The average price of tap water in cities around the world is about $2.3 per m³ but varies significantly by city and by country; for example, the price of high-quality water varies from a low of less than $1 per m³ to well over $6 per m³. For many cities in less developed countries, the price is less than $1 per m³ but the quality of the water can be much lower. The average price of a 500 mL bottle of drinking water is about $0.7, with a spread of $0.15–1.5.

The economics of desalinated water vary by technology, feedwater, energy used, and quality of water delivered; Table 3.6 summarises the current performance by technology. The MSF and MED technologies can provide the best quality water at a price of between about $1 and $2 per m³; the membrane technologies of RO and ED have a similar price, but the quality of water delivered is much lower, although still within that of natural freshwater resources.

Relatively low desalinated water prices are delivered when conventional, fossil fuel sources are used for thermal energy and to generate electricity. However, the price does not include the cost of the environmental externalities, be they gaseous emissions of carbon dioxide, sulphur, and nitrogen oxides, or damage to the local marine environment due to high-salinity water effluent from the desalination process. Externalities associated with sulphur and nitrogen oxides are normally addressed by investment in abatement technologies; however, this is not the case for CO_2 nor, currently, for the brine produced, although there are potential technology developments being considered to extract valuable chemicals from the latter waste stream.

Currently, the price of water goes up markedly when renewable sources are used to provide energy for the desalinated plants. When wind power is used, the price of water rises to between \$3 and over \$6 per m³ depending on the type of feedwater resources available; when solar photovoltaic technology is used to generate power, the price of water rises significantly to between \$8 and \$14 per m³, again depending on the feedwater type. However, the cost of renewable energy continues to fall, and this will feed into the cost of water as these technologies are integrated with desalination facilities at scale.

3.5.3 Desalination technology evolution

There are two ways of recognising innovation in technological evolution: s-curve analysis and learning curves. In the former, a key performance attribute of a technology is mapped against time and shows the improvements brought about by the industry, supported by its supply chain, technical institutions, and regulators. Technological evolution is slow in the early deployment of a technology as the industry gains valuable knowledge and understanding of the process. This is followed by a phase where there is rapid improvement in performance before slowing again to a plateau. It is possible that once a plateau is reached, there are further innovations that can lift performance to another level, and this signals the onset of a new s-curve for that technology.

Performance attributes for desalination technologies include cumulative installed plants and cumulative production capacity; s-curves can also be constructed for the average fleet capacity and maximum capacity of unit additions. When applied to the three main desalination technologies – RO, MSF, and MED – the performance attributes lie in the rapidly rising phase of their s-curves, showing that there has been very good progress in development over the last few decades.

The nature of this analysis is such that, so long as there is sufficient reliable data, it is possible to define the s-curve to the extent that it can be used to indicate the level of performance expected in the future. This is the case for the three main desalination technologies, and the analysis provides some helpful insights, but it is important to note that these are cumulative values and the actual number of plants in operation in any year will be lower because some plants would have retired at the end of their useful lives.

For example, in terms of cumulative installed capacity, the MSF and MED technologies are already at, or very close to, the plateau of their s-curves,

respectively, whereas that for RO will continue to rise, getting close to its plateau by the middle of the century. At the plateau, the cumulative number of MSF
plants built is about 1,600, and that for MED is about 2,400. RO deployment is
at another level, with the cumulative number of plants in 2020 at about 30,000,
rising to about 37,000 when this technology is close to its plateau in 2050.

In terms of cumulative production capacity, then, the s-curve analysis suggests that both the MSF and MED technologies are close to their plateau with
little growth over the coming decades. The analysis of the RO technology,
on the other hand suggests that its production capacity will continue to grow
significantly in the period to 2050.

'Learning curves' also provide insights into technology evolution. Traditionally, such curves have focused on capital cost or cost of production for
a technology and on how these decline with cumulative production through
the application of knowledge and experience gained; also captured in these
curves are the benefits associated with deploying larger plants, the so-called
'economies of scale'. Cost reduction via learning in industries such as energy
and chemicals also pass on these benefits to desalination plants.

One approach is to plot the data on a log-log scale, and the resultant
straight line reflects a constant decrease in cost of production. The slope of
the line is the Learning Coefficient (LC) and the steeper the line, the greater
the cost reduction. A Learning Rate (LR), defined as the fractional reduction
in cost for each doubling of cumulative production, is often used to describe
this process and is related to the LC by the simple equation $LR = (1-2^{(LC)})$.

There is good data on the specific investment cost, in $per m^3 per day, in
$2010, for the three mainstream commercial technologies over an extended
period. Analysis confirms there has been very good technology evolution for
the two thermal technologies MSF and MED with LR values of 33% and
36%, respectively; the LR value for membrane technology RO is just 15%,
and there is an expectation that there is more to come from this technology.

When the 'economies of scale' contribution to the cost reduction is excluded, the LR values for MSF, MED, and RO fall to 23%, 30%, and 12%,
respectively. However, it is worth noting that some of the biggest desalination
plants that have been built since this analysis was carried out are not included
and these have tended to use, in the main, RO technology; the LR value for
RO would need to be revised to take account of the economies of scale benefits associated with these very large plants.

3.6   Case studies involving the mainstream
commercial technologies

The global desalination industry is vibrant, and there is considerable ongoing
development, with new plants being added to the global fleet and expansion
phases raising the production capacity on many existing sites. The ten largest
desalination plants/sites are in the Middle East, where renewable freshwater

resources are very limited. These serve to illustrate the progress made by the industry over the last decade or so; they confirm the 'winning' technologies are RO, MSF, and MED. They also illustrate that, apart from increasing scale, the industry continues to innovate and combine technologies to optimise production, efficiency, and water quality.

The available basic information for the top ten desalination plants by size in 2021 is given in Table 3.7. It is worth noting that actual annual production will depend on several factors, such as demand, climate and renewable freshwater resources, and planned and unplanned outages.

All the top ten plants use seawater resources and have power stations close by to ensure security of energy supply; in fact, many new build projects have involved both power and desalination plants on the same site. Together, the capacity of these ten plants is over 7 million m³ per day, a remarkable achievement without which the water industries in these countries would face a huge challenge to meet the daily water needs of their citizens.

There are other plants that might have been included, such as the new 570,000 m³ per day Jubail 3B plant in Saudi Arabia, due to come into service in 2024. What is evident is that new production capacity continues to exceed that being decommissioned particularly in the Middle East.

Table 3.7 Ten largest desalination plants to-date

Name	Country	Capacity m³ per day	Technologies used	Commissioning date
Ras Al Kahir	Saudi Arabia	1,040,000	Multi-Stage Flash and Reverse Osmosis	2014
Al Taweelah	UAE	909,000	Reverse Osmosis	2023
Jubail Water and Power Company	Saudi Arabia	800,000	Multi-Effect Distillation	2022
Umm Al Quwain	UAE	683,000	Reverse Osmosis	2022
Jebel Ali M-Station	Dubai	636,000	Multi-Stage Flash	2019
Sorek	Israel	624,000	Reverse Osmosis	2013
Jubail 3A Independent Water Project	Saudi Arabia	600,000	Reverse Osmosis	2023
Shuaiba 3	Saudi Arabia	600,000	Reverse Osmosis	2025
Fujairah 2 Independent Water and Power Project	UAE	590,000	Multi-Stage Flash and Reverse Osmosis	2010
Sorek 2	Israel	580,000	Reverse Osmosis	2023

Source: Does size matter? Meet ten of the world's largest desalination plants, Aquatrade. com, 2021.

Note: Nameplate production capacity figures are shown, rounded to the nearest 1000 m³ per day.

Additional attributes of the top ten desalination plants

Not surprisingly, each desalination plant has slightly different attributes that distinguish it from the rest. For example, the overall cost and funding arrangements depend on whether a project is a standalone desalination plant or a capacity extension phase, the length of the water purchasing agreement, and the price of water.

1) *Ras Al Kahir plant in Saudi Arabia.* A hybrid plant with 8 MSF units and 17 RO units producing over 727,000 million m^3 per day and 109,000 million m^3 per day, respectively; the combined production can provide water for about 3 million people in the capital city of Riyadh. The site has a 2,650 MW power plant as part of the power and water complex; 1,350 MW of electricity and 25,000 m^3 per day of water are set aside for a refinery. The plant produces 1.5 m^3 of brine per m^3 of drinking water. The reported cost of the desalination complex is estimated at $US7 billion.

2) *Al Taweelah plant in the United Arab Emirates (UAE).* This plant has a low energy use of 3 kWh per m^3 water, with part of this energy met by photovoltaic technology. It benefits from a 30-year Water Purchase Agreement (WPA) and will deliver water at a low price of $0.49 per m^3. The large number of companies that were interested in participating in this project demonstrates the strong supply chain capability that has developed over the last few decades. This project will raise the contribution of RO technology in the UAE significantly.

3) *Jubail Water and Power Company plant in Saudi Arabia.* A joint power and water project, this plant was awarded a 20-year Power and Water Purchasing Agreement. The power is provided by 12 combined-cycle gas units with a total rated capacity of just over 2,700 MW.

4) *Umm Al Quwain plant in the UAE.* This plant cost $US 797 million and has been awarded a 35-year WPA. Detailed Environmental Impact Assessments (EIAs) were carried out with mitigating actions, such as the location of intake and outfall pipes at distances that minimise damage to the local marine environment. These, along with stakeholder consultations, are consistent with good practices in such infrastructure projects.

5) *Jebel Ali M-Station in Dubai.* This plant is part of the site where water desalination facilities have a total production capacity of over 2.2 million m^3 per day, the largest capacity in the world at a single site. The latest M-station has eight MSF units, each with an 80,000 m^3 per day capacity, and has been developed in phases over the years.

6) *Sorek desalination plant in Israel.* Feedwater is taken from two sea intake pipelines about 1.15 km offshore; a brine outfall pipeline was laid up to a depth of 20 m, approximately 1.85 km from shore. Electricity for the operation of the facility is provided by an independent power producer on the same site. The total investment was about $US400 million.

7) *Jubail 3A Independent Water Plant (IWP) in Saudi Arabia.* A project facilitated by Saudi Water Partnership Company (SWPC) to be delivered by

a consortium that will carry out all the activities – design, construction, commissioning, and operations, and maintenance – for the plant, including water storage and electrical facilities. The total capital cost is estimated at almost US$660 million, an investment made possible by a 25-year WPA.

8) *Shuaiba 3 IWP in Saudi Arabia.* Is being developed based on the principles established by SWPC: a 25-year WPA; 100% ownership of the project company by private investors; credit support provided by the Ministry of Finance covering all payments due under the WPA; and development of necessary electrical facilities, which are then transferred to National Grid SA ahead of the project's commercial operation date. A 60 MW solar photovoltaic plant will reduce consumption of grid electricity by 45%, and the switch from thermal to mechanical energy in the form of RO technology will reduce the overall power needed by 70%.

9) *Sorek 2 plant in Israel.* This is a Public-Private-Partnership (PPP) venture. It benefits from a 25-year agreement and delivers water at a low price of US$0.41 per m^3. This plant will produce 200 million m^3 of water output per year, increasing Israel's desalination capacity by 35%.

10) *Fujairah 2 Independent Water and Power Production (IWPP) plant in the UAE.* Uses two technologies for optimum performance: a MSF plant that delivers about 450,000 m^3 per day and a RO plant that produces about 140,000 m^3 per day. Power for the desalination facility is taken from a 2,000 MW power plant.

The attributes associated with these plants touch on many of the aspects highlighted above. It is also worth noting that these plants benefit from plentiful supplies of cheap fossil fuel energy in the Middle East, now including those in Israel, which is exploiting gas fields off its coast. The operating costs of these plants, then, are not necessarily representative of the industry.

Developers are keen to highlight the benefits of their projects, including, for example, the increasing use of renewable energy to power plants, particularly in the Middle East, where solar energy is plentiful. Detailed EIAs are also carried out and cover gaseous emissions from the use of oil and gas, directly in thermal processes such as MSF and MED, and indirectly via the electricity consumed in all desalination processes. Also covered in the EIAs is the brine from the plants that may potentially impact the marine environments local to the plant operations.

3.7 Summary key attributes of the mainstream technologies

A holistic view of mainstream technologies addresses several issues, including plant attributes, economics, operational metrics, energy matters, and environmental challenges. Table 3.8 below addresses the first three of these areas, while energy and environmental issues are discussed in Chapter 4.

Table 3.8 Key attribute values of the mainstream desalination technologies

Area	Attribute	Units/Aspect	RO	MSF	MED
Plant basics	Capacity range	1000 m³/day	<1–320	40–75	2–20
	Plant life	years	10–15	25–40	15–25
	Availability	%	92–96	96–98	96–98
Economics	Unit capital cost	$/m³/day	1313	1598	2000
	Cost of water	$/m³	0.26–0.54	0.56–1.75	0.52–1.01
Operation	Operating temperature	°C	Ambient	90–110	90–120
	Tons of feedwater per ton freshwater	Seawater feed	2–4	8–10	5–8
	Feedwater concentration	Seawater ppm	10,000–46,000	20,000–100,000	20,000–100,000
		Brackish water ppm	50–10,000	-	-
	Pure water recovery ratio	Seawater	0.42	0.22	0.25
		Brackish water	0.65	0.33	0.34
		River water	0.81	-	0.35
		Pure water	0.86	0.35	-
		Brine	0.19	0.09	0.12
		Wastewater	0.65	0.33	0.34
	Pure water quality	ppm	<500	<10	<10
	Maintenance frequency	Years	>4	2	2

Sources: Energy-water-environment nexus underpinning future desalination sustainability. Mohammad W. Shahzad et al., Desalination, Volume 413, pp52–62, 2017; Integration of wind energy and desalination systems: A Review study, Fransesca Greco et al., ResearchGate 2021; The state of desalination and brine production, Edward Jones et al., Science of Total Environment, Volume 657, p1343, 2019; Investigation of carbon footprints of three desalination technologies: Reverse Osmosis (RO), Multi-Stage Flash Distillation (MSF) and Multi-Effect Distillation (MED), Huyen Trang Do Thi and Andras Josef Toth, Periodica Polytechnica Chemical Engineering, 2023.

Summary key points

- Several factors play a role in the successful deployment of desalination in a country, from the nature of freshwater needs to the price of water to the consumer. Each country exhibits a unique set of conditions.
- The desalination sector has matured over the last 60 years or so and continues to innovate. It has a good bedrock of knowledge and experience for future growth, and there is an expectation that this growth will be realised.
- Desalination projects are complex and involve a range of stakeholders from across the political, industrial, and local community spectrums The industry must address the concerns and needs of all stakeholders for the successful development of its projects.

- There are 193 member countries of the UN and the vast majority of which have desalination facilities. The Middle East and North Africa region accounts for almost 48% of the estimated global desalination production capacity of just over 95 million m³ per day; this region hosts the ten largest plants/sites in the world, one of which has broken the 1 million m³ per day barrier.

- The winning technologies have emerged, with RO dominating the sector and with significant contributions made by MSF and MED. There is a growing tendency to have two technologies on the same site to improve overall performance.

- The cost of desalinated water is dependent on several factors, including the technology adopted, the nature of the feedwater, the type and quantity of energy used, and the quality of the water produced. The benchmark technology is RO using brackish feedwater, which produces water at a cost of about $0.9 per m³. This value rises to $3.0 per m³ and $8 per m³ if wind and solar photovoltaic energy is used, respectively.

4 Energy and environment

Energy and the environment are key issues for the desalination industry, with the former being an essential part of the process and the latter a key consideration for local communities.

4.1 Energy provision for water

Energy is needed in all aspects of the water sector: abstraction, water treatment, distribution, and desalination. Electricity is the main energy carrier, and the International Energy Agency (IEA) estimated the quantity consumed by the water sector at almost 825 TWh in 2014, projecting a rise to over 1,475 TWh in 2040. Electricity consumption in desalination was estimated at about 40 TWh, or 5% of the total in 2014, and was projected to increase rapidly to 345 TWh in 2040, or just under a quarter of the total consumption for all water industry activities in that year. Such growth has major implications for the energy sector and for the environment that need to be addressed.

4.1.1 Energy and the desalination process

Energy, in its various forms, is a critical component of the desalination process without which there would be no pure water. However, it also contributes significantly to the overall cost of producing this water, and it can pollute the environment, the extent depending on the feedwater source and the technology employed. There are five forms of energy that can be used for desalination: thermal, electrical, mechanical, chemical, and nuclear. The first four of these are already being exploited directly in desalination, and the fifth, nuclear energy, can be used indirectly by its provision of large quantities of electricity to the grid network in those countries that have both desalination and nuclear plants.

The oldest form of energy used in desalination is thermal, with eight technologies relying on this source, including the Multi-Stage Flash (MSF), Multi-Effect Distillation (MED) and Thermal Vapour Compression (TVC).

DOI: 10.4324/9781003334224-4

Mechanical energy is applied in Reverse Osmosis (RO), the dominant technology today, and four other technologies. Two technologies are based on electrical energy, including Electrodialysis (ED), and just one technology exploits chemical energy. There are also hybrid desalination plants that utilise two technologies on the site to improve the overall efficiency of the process and the quality of water produced, and here, both thermal and mechanical energy are used. Of course, all desalination sites use electricity, for example, for pumps and other equipment, and this form of energy is arguably the most important energy source.

4.1.2 Energy consumption by technology

The amount of energy used, electrical or thermal, depends on several factors, including the technology adopted, the efficiency of the plant, the feedwater available, and the quality of the water produced. These factors, then, result in a spread of energy values for each of the main technologies rather than a single value, as shown in Table 4.1.

The three main thermal technologies use large quantities of energy when compared to those technologies that use mechanical energy. Those technologies based on the latter benefit from using electrical energy, which is gradually

Table 4.1 Energy characteristics of the main desalination technologies

Process	Technology	Thermal energy kJ/kg	Electrical equivalent of thermal energy kWh/m^3	Electrical energy kWh/m^3	Total electrical energy equivalent kWh/m^3
Thermal	Multi-Stage Flash	190–390	15.8–32.5	4–6	19.8–38.5
	Multi-Effect Distillation	230–390	19.1–32.5	1.5–2.5	20.6–35.0
	Thermal Vapour Compression	145–390	12.1–32.5	1.5–2.5	13.6–35.0
Mechanical	Seawater Reverse Osmosis			3–6	3–6
	Brackish water Reverse Osmosis			1.5–2.5	1.5–2.5
	Mechanical Vapour Compression			6–12	6–12
	Electrodialysis			2.6–5.5	2.6–5.5

Source: Integration of Wind Energy and Desalination Systems: A Review Study, Francesca Greco et al., ResearchGate, 2021.

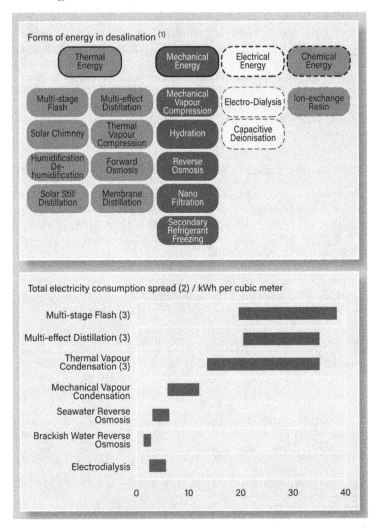

Figure 4.1 Desalination technologies by energy used

Sources: (1), A Review of Water Desalination Technologies, Curto et al., Applied Sciences, Volume 11, p670, 2021; (2), Integration of Wind Energy and Desalination Systems: A Review Study, Francesca Greca et al., ResearchGate, December 2021.

Note: (3), The sum of the thermal energy used, expressed in electricity equivalent, and actual electricity consumed in the process.

being decarbonised in the drive to reduce carbon dioxide emissions from the power generation sector. The relatively low electricity consumption values also help explain why RO has emerged as the dominant technology being deployed today, particularly in those countries where indigenous sources of fossil energy are less readily available.

4.1.3 Global electricity consumption by the desalination industry

It is possible to estimate the energy consumption of the global desalination sector based on the production of pure water by technology employed. The three main technologies, RO, MSD, and MED, delivered about 66, 17, and 7 million m^3 water per day, respectively, out of a total 95 million m^3 per day in 2020; about 6 million m^3 per day was delivered by Nanofiltration and Electrodialysis. Assuming average electricity consumption values per m^3 of pure water produced by these technologies, it is possible to estimate a total electricity consumption by the desalination sector of about 140 TWh in 2020; not surprisingly, most of this electricity is used by RO facilities since this technology produced an estimated 70% of the world's desalinated water in 2020.

An estimate of the thermal energy consumed is also important. Expressed in terms of electricity equivalents, the total consumed by the main thermal technologies of MSF, MED, and TVC amounts to about 225 TWh in 2020; this is due to the relatively high energy intensity associated with these processes, although the three technologies delivered just 25% of the total daily production.

It is worth putting the estimated energy used in desalination into context. If electricity alone is considered, the global value of 140 TWh in 2020 is comparable to the total consumed in Argentina (143 TWh) or Pakistan (138 TWh). Alternatively, this can be compared to the electricity produced by certain technologies that year; for example, hydroelectric schemes in Norway produced 141 TWh, electricity generation by natural gas in Italy was 136 TWh, nuclear power in South Korea delivered 160 TWh, and renewables in Japan generated 126 TWh. The electricity consumed by the sector, then, is significant and is even more so if the thermal energy is also considered.

4.1.4 Renewable energy used for desalination

The deployment of renewable technologies around the world is an important contributor to the decarbonisation of the energy sector. The progress made in the sector over the last 25 years is remarkable, with the 'winning' technologies of wind and solar emerging into the mainstream. There are many contributing factors for this success, from innovation and technology development to political ambition for the sector underpinned by generous financial incentives in the early stages of deployment.

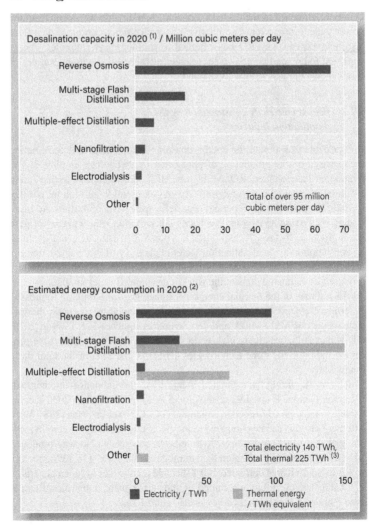

Figure 4.2 Energy consumption by the global desalination industry

Source: (1), Integration of Wind Energy and Desalination Systems: A Review Study, Francesca Greco et al., ResearchGate, December 2021.

Note: (2), Uses averages i.e. mean between high and low values quoted in Source (1) above – in kWh/cubic meter – to estimate total energy used; the 'Other' category is assumed to be Thermal Vapour Condensation for the purposes of this simple analysis; (3), in electricity equivalent.

Renewable costs have declined markedly as the technologies have been deployed at scale by a maturing global supply chain; onshore wind costs have declined by a factor of three over the last 20 years or so, while those for solar photovoltaic (PV) have fallen more dramatically, by a factor of ten. The cost of electricity from these two technologies is now comparable with, and in some cases lower than, that of mainstream, conventional generation technologies that use coal, gas, and nuclear. However, renewable technologies continue to be hampered by their intermittency and the lack of large-scale storage media that would increase their utility. Nonetheless, wind and solar capacity in 2020 amounted to over 700 GW for each technology; the combined total of about 1,440 GW for these two technologies is already greater than the 1,360 GW of hydroelectric schemes around the world.

Interest in linking renewable electricity with desalination has grown over the years due, in part, to the fact that many countries that suffer from freshwater shortages also have significant indigenous renewables resources to exploit. But there are other reasons for using renewables and desalination together. As indicated above, renewable costs have fallen significantly, particularly those that have been deployed at scale like onshore and offshore wind and solar Photo-Voltaic (PV); and unlike electricity production, water can be stored and used when needed and this means the intermittency of wind and solar is less of a problem. In fact, viewed differently, the production of desalinated water is one way of 'storing' renewable energy.

Wind and solar technologies contribute to the low-carbon energy sector alongside hydroelectricity, nuclear, geothermal, and to a much lesser extent the ocean technologies of wave and tidal stream. All technologies have positive and negative attributes, and it is possible to compare their performance against a set of criteria, as shown in Table 4.2.

So, for example, wind and solar generation are well placed when assessed against cost competitiveness and technology maturity. However, if reliability

Table 4.2 Current status of low carbon technologies

Low carbon technology	Technology development	Consistency of electricity supply	Location options	Cost competitiveness with mainstream fossil technologies	Electricity provision for desalination
Hydro	Mature	Good	Limited	Medium	Through grid
Wind	Developed	Intermittent	Many	High	Yes
Solar	Developed	Intermittent	Many	High	Yes
Geothermal	Mature	High	Very limited	Medium	No
Ocean	Early stage	Predictable	Limited	Low	No
Nuclear	Mature	High	Many	Medium	Through grid

Source: Author's assessment.

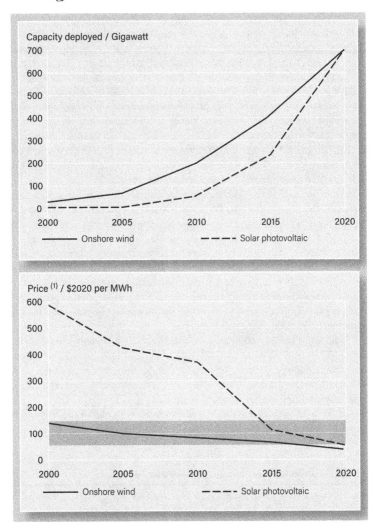

Figure 4.3 Renewable energy use in desalination increasingly viable

Source: Climate Change 2022: Mitigation of Climate Change, Working Group III contribution to the Sixth Assessment Report of the Intergovernmental Panel on Climate Change, 2022.

Note: (1), Band shows cost of fossil fuel electricity.

Table 4.3 Matching commercial renewable options to mainstream desalination technologies

Technology	Energy option	Desalination technology
Wind	Electricity	Reverse Osmosis
Solar	Thermal (to generate electricity)	Reverse Osmosis
	Thermal (collectors provide heat)	Multi-Stage Flash, Multi-Effect Distillation
	Photovoltaic (electricity)	Reverse Osmosis
Geothermal	Thermal (provide heat)	Multi-Stage Flash, Multi-Effect Distillation
	Generate electricity	Reverse Osmosis

Source: Linear Fresnel Concentrator with dual energy solar tracking Application: Seawater desalination, Mohamed Oulhazzan et al., European Journal of Scientific Research, 142, pp72–80, 2016.

of supply and high volumes of electricity generation are important and grid transmission is available, then both nuclear and hydroelectricity, if available, would be the preferred choices. On the other hand, if relatively low technical capability is needed to deploy, operate, and maintain the technology and the ability to site plants in many locations are important criteria, then wind and solar generation would, once again, score highly.

For these reasons, there is progress in combining renewable electricity and desalination, and potential options are shown in Table 4.3. As indicated above, nuclear power and hydroelectricity are low-carbon sources deployed in many countries that have desalination plants, and this attribute is reflected in the carbon content of electricity provided to desalination plants via the grid by utilities. A key development is the recent commissioning of nuclear power stations in the Middle East, and these will help decarbonise the electricity sector in those countries.

Such combinations will gather pace as members of the Global Clean Water Desalination Alliance (GCWDA) deliver their targets under a new initiative. The growing dominance of RO in the desalination sector suggests renewable technologies are well placed to deliver the electricity needed for this technology.

Global Clean Water Desalination Alliance

The GCWDA set several goals for renewable technologies in terms of the percentage of energy supplied to new desalination plants at milestone dates over the next two decades. The target was set at 20% of the total energy consumed by new operational facilities in the period 2020–2025; the target is higher at 40% for new operational plants in the period 2026–2030, 60% for the period

2031–2035, and 80% for all new operational plants post-2035. This is an ambitious initiative which, if successful, will largely decarbonise the sector.

Founded by the International Desalination Association, the GCWDA has well over 140 members in 38 countries covering all the inhabited continents. Most of the membership (56%) is from industry, including the energy and water sector, the desalination sector, and supply chain companies; 26% are research and development organisations; 24% are governmental organisations; and 8% are international organisations. With this geographical, commercial, institutional, and technical reach, the GCWDA is a highly credible group, recognised on the Climate Change Platform of the United Nations Environment Programme, and well-placed to deliver on the targets agreed.

Case study in the global clean water desalination alliance initiative

Saudi Arabia has emerged as a prominent country actor in the desalination sector, with its production capacity growing by a factor of over 2.5 in the period 2010–2020. The country is an important member of the GCWDA, and it is possible to assess what will be needed for it to meet its goal under this initiative.

The estimated renewable generation needed will depend on the projected desalination production capacity in, for example, the period 2020–2025, and this in turn can be estimated from the population growth and the overall per capita consumption. The population is expected to grow from 35 million to over 38 million in the five-year period. In one scenario (A), the per capita consumption over the five-year period can be assumed to remain at the same level as that in 2020; the result is an annual production capacity *increase* of about 220 million m^3 of water by the end of the five-year period in 2025. In a second scenario (B), the per capita demand can be assumed to continue to grow with development, say at 3% per annum, and this results in an *increased* annual production capacity of about 615 million m^3 of water by 2025.

Assuming RO technology is used going forward and the electricity required to deliver the extra production capacity is about 4 kWh per m^3 of water, this results in a total additional electricity demand of 875 GWh and 2,465 GWh for scenarios A and B, respectively. To meet the aims of the GCWDA, then, requires that 20% of this generation must be met using renewable generation, which amounts to 175 GWh and 475 GWh for scenarios A and B, respectively. Further, assume that this electricity will be met by solar PV technology since Saudi Arabia has already deployed about 400 MW in the country and that a load factor of 24% is possible based on existing solar PV in that region.

Using the information above, a simple analysis suggests that the electricity required to meet the GCWDA target in Saudi Arabia would require an

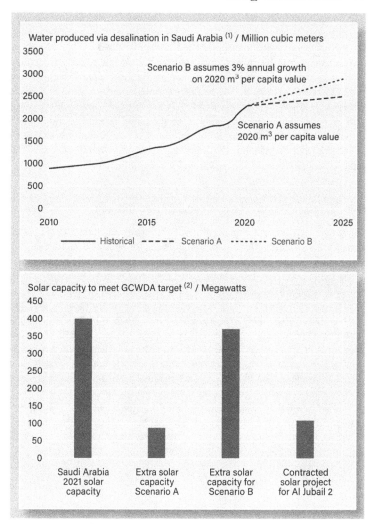

Figure 4.4 Meeting the Global Clean Water Desalination Alliance target

Sources: (1), Saudi Arabia's desalination plant water production 2010-2019, Statista, 2022; Saudi Arabia: Total population from 2017 to 2027, Statista, 2022.

Note: (2), Solar capacity calculated from generation data in BP Statistical Review 2022; GCWDA, the Global Clean Water Desalination Alliance, has set a target of 20% of all new desalination plants between 2020 and 2025 to be powered by renewables (see text for Scenario A and B).

additional 90 MW and 370 MW of solar PV capacity for scenarios A and B, respectively. This is well within the capability of the country, bearing in mind the financial and technical resources that can be mobilised.

An example of the move to renewables driven by the GCWDA initiative is the Al Jubail 2 water desalination plant on the east coast of Saudi Arabia. Here, 110 MW of solar PV technology and the associated electrical infrastructure (a 380 kV substation and 173 km of overhead transmission lines) will be deployed to provide electricity to the plant. There will also be both ground-mounted and floating PV deployment. At a reported investment of about $320 million, this initiative alone will go some way towards Saudi Arabia meeting its commitments under the GCWDA initiative.

4.2   Environmental consequences of desalination

There are environmental impacts associated with all industrial processes throughout their lifecycle, and this is the same for desalination plants. They begin with the siting and construction of a plant, continuing throughout their long operational lives, and ultimately to their decommissioning and deconstruction at the end-of-life.

The physical footprint of the infrastructure associated with water management is significant and requires considerable resources to be expended. Some desalination plants may be sited well away from the coast, and this has consequences in the form of the emissions from the electricity needed to transport large volumes of water safely over long distances. Seawater desalination plants also require careful siting of the large intake and outfall water pipes to minimise the physical impact on the local marine environment.

All industrial processes inevitably have waste associated with their operations, and these need to be addressed; once again, desalination is no different. There are two main waste streams: those associated with gas emissions resulting from the combustion of fossil fuels, either directly in the process or indirectly in the production of electricity used in the process; a second and more contentious issue is the production of water with enhanced salinity (brine), along with toxic chemicals such as chlorine and copper in the desalination process, and these must be managed.

The nature of the gaseous emissions will depend on the hydrocarbon fuel used but will always include CO_2; to these might be added nitrogen oxides and, when coal and, to a lesser extent, oil are used, sulphur oxides. Carbon dioxide is a global pollutant because it has a long lifetime and readily mixes throughout the atmosphere. Nitrogen and sulphur oxides are regional pollutants because they are more readily scavenged in the lower atmosphere (troposphere). There has been good progress in reducing all gaseous pollutants from power stations over the last few decades by increasing efficiency and fitting nitrogen and sulphur abatement technologies.

4.2.1 Carbon dioxide emissions

CO_2 emissions arise from the combustion of hydrocarbons used to provide thermal energy and in the production of electricity. Such emissions contribute to climate change, and as with all industrial processes, there is a concerted effort to decarbonise the desalination process. As indicated above, this can be achieved through the choice of technology, efficiency improvements, and in the provision of low-carbon energy. It is important to establish the scale of the issue in the first instance and, by doing so, provide a baseline against which to monitor progress in decarbonisation.

The three mainstream technologies of MSF, MED, and RO, then, all contribute to CO_2 emissions, the level is dependent on a number of issues: the hydrocarbons used in the energy supply, the efficiency of both the desalination plant and power station involved, the load factor of the desalination plants, the nature of the feedwater available since this determines the effort needed to produce pure water of the required quality, and the distance to the coast, and beyond into the sea, where the intake and outfall pipes for the seawater and brine produced are located, respectively. For these reasons, estimates of carbon emissions vary significantly between technologies, and it is appropriate to consider ranges when estimating carbon emissions by technology and the total burden on the environment.

The most carbon-intensive of the mainstream technologies is MSF, with a range of 15.6–25.0 kgm CO_2 per m^3 of pure water produced; this is not surprising since it uses both thermal energy and electricity and operates at high temperatures. MED is similarly carbon intensive for the same reasons, with a range of 7.0–17.6 kgmCO_2 per m^3. RO has a small range of lower values in terms of carbon intensity, estimated at 1.7–2.5 kgmCO_2 per m^3, largely because it operates at ambient temperatures and only uses electricity.

Using the estimated daily global pure water production capacity in 2020 of about 95 million m^3, and the best-case scenario of the low emission factors for each technology highlighted above, provides an indicative value for the global CO_2 emission of 175 million tonnes from the desalination sector in 2020. To put these best-case emissions into context, they are comparable to the total CO_2 emissions of, say, the Netherlands or Argentina, which were 176 and 164 million tonnes, respectively, in 2020.

The largest contributor to the sector emissions of CO_2 is the MSF plant, with emissions of at least 100 million tonnes, despite a low pure water production capacity of about 17 million m^3; the next largest is the RO plant, with emissions of 40 million tonnes but with the largest production capacity of about 62 million tonnes m^3 water, and MED, with emissions of about 15 million tonnes from the production of 6 million m^3 water.

To get an accurate value for CO_2 emissions from the sector, requires a plant-by-plant estimate to be carried out so that their individual circumstances are considered. Also, a lifecycle analysis rather than an operational

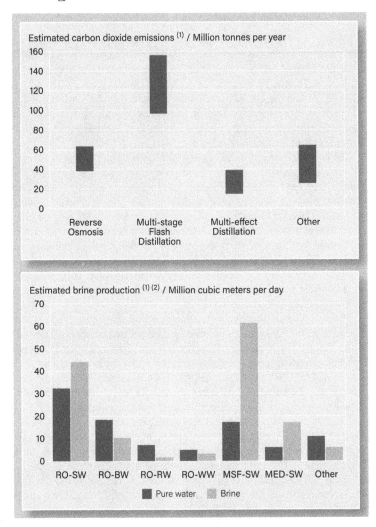

Figure 4.5 Carbon dioxide emissions and brine production

Sources: Energy-water-environment nexus underpinning future desalination sustainability, M.W. Shahzad et al., Desalination, Volume 413, pp52–62, 2017; The state of desalination and brine production, E. Jones et al., Science of Total Environment, 657, p1343, 2019.

Notes: (1), See text; (2), RO, Reverse Osmosis; SW, Sea Water; BW, Brackish Water; Rw, River Water; WW, Waste Water; MSF, Multi-Stage Flash Distillation; MED, Multi-Effect Distillation.

assessment is increasingly being carried out in, for example, the energy sector to provide a more holistic approach and better reflect the environmental impact of plants. The same approach will likely be carried out for desalination plants in the future.

Almost 50% of the global water production capacity is in the Middle East and North Africa region, and these plants tend to use thermal energy, which means that most of the CO_2 emissions will be from this region. The next three major regions, in terms of size of production capacity, are East Asia and the Pacific, North America, and Western Europe, and it is reasonable to assume that they also contribute significantly to the sector's CO_2 emissions.

4.2.2 Brine production

An important metric for the water industry is the Total Dissolved Solids (TDS) which is the amount of organic and inorganic materials, such as metals, minerals, salts, and ions, dissolved in water and expressed as milligrams (mg) per litre or parts per million (ppm). Total dissolved solids come from many sources, both natural and man-made. Natural sources of TDS include springs, lakes, rivers, plants, and soil; human activity can also produce TDS in water, for example, through pesticides and herbicides from agricultural runoff and chlorine from water treatment plants. Drinking water has a recommended maximum value of less than 500 ppm, with a value greater than 1,000 ppm deemed unsafe.

Brine is water with a salinity above that of the feedwater resource used and is the waste product of the desalination process. This waste has a TDS value of up to 65,000 ppm, which is almost twice the value of about 35,000 ppm for the seawater resources being exploited. Brackish water typically has a value of just 2,000 ppm.

The environmental impact of brine on marine life is still not well understood, and there is an urgent need for monitoring and research over a long period because desalination plants have a lifetime of 20–35 years and their size continues to grow; their potential to damage marine ecosystems, then, is considerable. Also, the total number of operational plants is expected to grow significantly over the next 30 years, putting further pressure on marine environments local to the plants.

In the best-case scenario, there is an expectation that a good engineering solution would result in the brine waste stream being heavily diluted when deposited in the seawater, so that the effect on marine life is minimal. However, the salinity and density of brine is considerably higher than those of seawater, and this change in the salinity of the sea in the proximity of the desalination plant can damage the local marine ecosystem. The most significant impact on marine life, such as fish, plankton, algae, seagrass, and other marine life, is the osmotic 'stress' caused by a sudden change in the solute concentration around a cell of a species. This causes a change in the movement of water across the cell membrane, increasing the pressure within the cell, a process that can ultimately result in the long-term extinction of marine species in the area around the desalination plant outfall pipes.

There are attempts to address the potential environmental damage of brine by converting this waste to useful products by well-known chemical processes, although this has yet to be put into practice at a desalination site. For example, the brine waste can be processed to yield chemicals such as sodium hydroxide (NaOH) or hydrochloric acid (HCl). The former could be used to pre-treat seawater going into the desalination plant, which changes the acidity of the water and helps to prevent fouling of membranes, a major cause of interruptions and failures in RO technology. Hydrochloric acid could also be made on site from the waste brine and could be used for cleaning parts of the desalination plant; it is also widely used in chemical processes.

A commercial operation involving chemical production of this kind would diminish the environmental impact of the brine waste and enhance the economic viability of the desalination process. A barrier is the cost of both the equipment and the energy needed for the processes.

4.2.3   *Brine production by technology*

The water recovery ratio of mainstream technologies varies depending on the feedwater available. In simple terms, about 1.4 m^3 of brine is produced for every m^3 of pure water produced by the RO-seawater (RO-SW) combination, falling to about 0.2 m^3 of brine per m^3 of freshwater by the RO-river water (RO-RW) combination; these values compare very favourably with the MSF-SW and MED-SW values, where 3.5 and 3.0 m^3 of brine are produced for every m^3 of pure water.

The global brine production was estimated at over 140 million m^3 for 2020, with over 70% of the total in the Middle East and North Africa region and the next largest contributor of over 10% in East Asia and the Pacific; this is not surprising since brine-intensive MSF and MED technologies play an important role in these regions. All other regions produced single-digit volumes of brine, which together accounted for less than 20% of the total in 2020.

In terms of technology-feedwater combinations, MSF-SW dominated with an estimated 60 million m^3 of brine from the production of just over 17 million m^3 of pure water in 2020; the second thermal technology, MED-SW, produced almost 17 million m^3 but from less than 6 million m^3 of pure water. The combination of RO-SW produced just under 44 million m^3 of brine but from a total production of over 32 million m^3 of pure water; all the RO-feedwater combinations together produced 58 million m^3 of brine from 62 million m^3 of pure water.

Once produced, the brine waste must be managed, and this is achieved, in the main, by emitting it into the marine environment, where natural dilution can minimise its impact. An important consideration, then, is the siting of the desalination plant. An estimated 50% of the brine produced is in plants located less than 1 km from the coast, and a further 30% of the brine is produced by plants between 1 and 10 km from the coast. Plants that lie beyond 10 km, accounting for over 20% of the total brine produced, clearly face considerable challenges in disposing of the brine waste.

4.2.4 Summary key attributes of the mainstream technologies

The energy and environmental attributes of RO now make it the preferred technology, as demonstrated by the metrics in Table 4.4 below. However, it is important that other aspects are considered, including those attributes summarised in Table 3.7 in Chapter 3, for a holistic view of desalination technologies.

Table 4.4 Key energy and environment metrics for the three mainstream technologies

Area	Attribute	Feedwater	Units	RO	MSF	MED
Energy	Energy Source			Mechanical	Thermal	Thermal
	Electricity consumption		kWh per m³	5–9	4–6	1.5–2.5
	Thermal energy consumption		kJ per kg	None	190–390	230–390
	Electrical equivalent of thermal energy		kWh per m³	None	9.5–19.5	5.0–8.5
Environment	Discharge temperature		°C (above ambient)	0	10–15	10–15
	Carbon dioxide emissions		kg per m³	1.7–2.8	15.6–25.0	7.0–17.6
	Ratio brine to freshwater	Seawater		1.35	3.54	2.97
		Brackish water		0.55	-	-
		River water		0.21	-	-
		Waste water		0.59	-	-

Sources: Energy-water-environment nexus underpinning future desalination sustainability. Mohammad W. M.W. Shahzad et al., Desalination, Volume 413, pp52–62, 2017; Integration of wind energy and desalination systems: A Review study, Fransesca Greco et al., ResearchGate 2021; The state of desalination and brine production, Edward Jones et al., Science of Total Environment, 657, p1343, 2019; Investigation of carbon footprints of three desalination technologies: Reverse Osmosis (RO), Multi-Stage Flash Distillation (MSF) and Multi-Effect Distillation (MED), Huyen Trang Do Thi and Andras Josef Toth Periodica Polytechnica Chemical Engineering, 2023.

Summary key points

- The nature and quantity of energy used is an important factor in the desalination sector because of its contribution to the cost of freshwater provided to the consumer, and the implications for the environment.
- Electricity is the dominant energy carrier, although thermal energy also plays an important role in two of the three mainstream technologies and, crucially, in the Middle East, where water scarcity is high and oil and gas supplies are plentiful.
- The GCWDA initiative has member organisations in 38 countries and has set a goal for 20% of the energy supplied to new desalination plants to be powered by renewables between 2020 and 2025 and more ambitious targets thereafter.
- Gaseous emissions from energy use include the global pollutant CO_2 and the local and regional pollutants nitrogen and sulphur oxides. An estimate of CO_2 emissions associated with the global desalination industry amounted to at least 175 million tonnes in 2020, comparable to the total emissions of countries like the Netherlands or Argentina.
- An estimated 140 million cubic metres of brine waste was produced in 2020, with over 70% in the Middle East and North Africa region.
- RO was the least polluting technology per cubic metre of pure water of all the three mainstream technologies.

5 Desalination in selected countries

Desalination is an essential technology in many parts of the world, primarily for the provision of drinking water but also to support agriculture and industrial activity.

5.1 Context

The main drivers for water use and desalination were discussed in Chapter 2, with population and economic growth prominent, along with the impacts of climate change in the form of rising temperatures, decreasing rainfall in some regions, and increased extreme weather events. These developments have put pressure on water resources in many parts of the world, and the situation is expected to worsen in the coming years and decades. In Chapters 3 and 4, important aspects of the desalination industry were explored, demonstrating the attributes and complexities associated with this technology. They included, for example, the nature and scale of the technologies being adopted, the feedwater options, economics and water pricing, energy and environmental issues, and the sectors being serviced by the industry.

The regions of the world most affected include the Middle East and North Africa, the Mediterranean countries, parts of Europe, North and South America, and Asia and Oceania; island states in these regions are particularly vulnerable because of their isolation. The countries selected within each region include Saudi Arabia, Israel, and Morocco in the Middle East and North Africa, Spain and the UK in Europe, parts of USA and Chile in North and South America respectively, China in East Asia, and Australia in Oceania, Cyprus, part of Europe and in the Mediterranean, is used to illustrate the unique problems of a sizeable island state.

5.2 Country case studies

Many of the key country metrics were introduced in Chapter 2 and are summarised briefly below to provide the overall context for the case studies. Each country has its own physical characteristics that help determine its water use, for example,

DOI: 10.4324/9781003334224-5

its size and natural resources. The size, density, and growth rate of its population are important, as is the population distribution between urban and rural areas, and the Human Development Index (HDI) is a helpful measure of a country's development. It is also important to note that there can be significant differences within a country; for example, those that occupy a large land mass, such as the USA, China, and Australia, or their geography and location provide nuanced weather conditions, such as those that occur in Chile and the UK.

The economic activity of a country is an important driver of water consumption. The Gross Domestic Product (GDP) is a good overall indicator of the size and health of a country's economy over a set period, usually over a quarter or year; it is also used to compare the size of different economies over time. GDP can be defined in several ways, the most common of which is the total value of goods and services produced in a country. GDP per capita is also an important indicator.

The energy and water sectors are intimately linked. Water plays an important role in mainstream fossil and nuclear electricity generation plants, while the water sector needs electricity in large quantities to transport water around a country's infrastructure and to operate treatment plants. Desalination is an energy-intensive and expensive activity, particularly for those countries that have few indigenous fossil fuel resources. For this reason, and because of the need to decarbonise their energy sector, countries are beginning to exploit their renewable resources. The Global Clean Water Desalination Alliance (GCWDA) was founded by the International Desalination Association and includes members from across the energy spectrum. The alliance has set a first goal of 20% of the energy needs of new desalination plants to be powered by renewables in the period 2020–2025, with further, more ambitious targets over the next 10 years.

Climate change is recognised as a key driver for changes in weather, with implications for rainfall patterns and increased frequency of extreme events. There is a keen interest in the carbon intensity of a country's electricity generation sector – the carbon emissions per unit of electricity produced – since this plays an important role in desalination. The Climate Risk Index (CRI) is a method for assessing the extent to which countries are affected by extreme weather events such as droughts, heat waves, wildfires, storms, and floods, and is a measure of both human and economic losses. Each country is ranked in a particular year or over a long period of time against about 180 countries worldwide. For example, Japan, which ranked 1st in 2018 and 4th in 2019, was amongst the most affected countries by extreme weather events in recent years, although it ranked an average 57th when assessed across the period 2000–2019. This analysis is helpful in identifying those countries most at risk and needing support from the international community to help mitigate the worst effects of climate change.

Each country has its own unique characteristics. This will also be the case for the social, economic, and environmental drivers for the key freshwater metrics discussed in Chapter 2. The level of water stress in any country is reported as *freshwater withdrawals as a proportion of available freshwater resources*. There are various levels of water stress: extremely high if the ratio of withdrawals to supply is >80% and low if the ratio is <10%. The use of freshwater water resources also varies significantly from one country to another. In many countries, agriculture dominates water withdrawals, while in others, the domestic sector or industry plays a prominent role.

Chapter 3 introduced the dimensions of desalination, those that are related to its deployment and those that are related to the industry. The country case studies presented below, together, illustrate all the dimensions of desalination. Each case study begins with a brief country summary.

5.2.1 Saudi Arabia

Saudi Arabia has very low renewable water resources and is depleting its ancient aquifers; it is currently using 10 times its renewable water resources. Agriculture is the major consumer, with almost 70% of the water used for this sector. Desalination is a mature industry in the country and has a current capacity of about 6.6 million m^3 per day, which accounts for 6.3% of the world's desalination production capacity. This industry produces enough water to meet about 65% of the country's drinking water needs. The dominant technology is Multi-Stage Flash (MSF) desalination, with close to 80% of the total, made possible by the ready availability of cheap indigenous fossil fuels.

Context for desalination

Saudi Arabia is a country with a land area of 2.15 million square km, the 13th largest in the world. The country has coastlines with both the Red Sea and the Persian Gulf. Its population has increased by almost a factor of nine within a human lifetime, from just 4 million in 1960 to 36 million in 2021. Its urban population has also increased significantly over this period, from just 30% of the total in 1960 to 85% in 2020; the capital city, Riyadh, has a population of about 4.2 million people. In terms of the CRI, Saudi Arabia ranked 75th out of 182 countries in 2019, which is worse than its ranking of 111th for the period 2000–2019.

Saudi Arabia is very well endowed with fossil fuel resources. Its proved oil reserves amount to 300 billion barrels, or over 17% of the world total; its production was 11 million barrels per day in 2021. The country also has 6 trillion m^3 of proved gas reserves, or 3% of the world's total. These resources are a major part of the economy, with exports in hydrocarbons, chemicals, plastics, and manufacturing materials. The country is also well endowed with renewable resources, and it is very well placed to exploit solar energy with some of the highest radiation levels in the world. Also, the technical potential for wind energy deployment is beyond leading countries such as the USA, UK, and Germany.

The wealth of the country, then, relies very heavily on its energy resources, with fossil fuels currently dominating. However, agriculture is also an important sector, even though only 2% of the country's land area is considered arable; the main agricultural crops include dates and fruit. Saudi Arabia has an HDI of 0.875, well within the 'very high' Human Development Category, and is the 35th ranked country in the world.

Water resources and demand

While Saudi Arabia is one of the leading countries for energy resources in the world, it is, arguably, the least well-endowed when it comes to renewable water resources at 71 m³ per capita; it is an arid country with very low rainfall and no running freshwater. Its annual freshwater withdrawals amount to a staggering 900% of internal resources, with total water consumed in the country of 15.4 billion cubic metres (m³) in 2019.

Daily water consumption for the urban sector was 279 litres per capita per day in 2019, amounting to over 9.6 million m³ per day; the total for this sector in that year was 3.5 billion m³, or 23% of the total water consumed. This is expected to rise in future years as the population continues to grow, even with efficiency gains in water use. Agriculture continues to use the most water resources, 10.5 billion m³, or 68% of the total water consumed in 2019. Industry uses the least water, just 1.4 bm³, or 9% of the total.

A major source of freshwater are aquifers, which were filled thousands of years ago and at one time containing an estimated 500 cubic kilometres (km³) of water. However, exploitation of this resource, primarily for agriculture and farming, amounts to about 20 km³ each year, and this extraction rate has severely depleted these natural resources; some estimates suggest that as much as 80% of the water in these 'ancient' aquifers has gone.

Desalination in Saudi Arabia

The need for pure water to meet the needs of a growing population in Saudi Arabia and the development of a desalination industry to produce it, is not a recent development. Desalination technology has been used since the 1950s and has grown significantly over the last seven decades, to the extent that the country now leads the world in terms of deployment. In 2019, the industry produced 2,256 million m³ or 6.2 million m³ per day, meeting 65% of the country's urban water needs; this is 2.5 times that produced just ten years earlier. The remaining 35% needed for urban water consumption is from aquifers.

In 2020, Saudi Arabia had 33 desalination plants built along the Red Sea coast, and all exploit seawater. Saudi Arabia accounts for around 20% of the world's desalinated water production. The main techniques used are Multi-Stage Flash (MSF), Reverse Osmosis (RO) and Multi-Effect Desalination

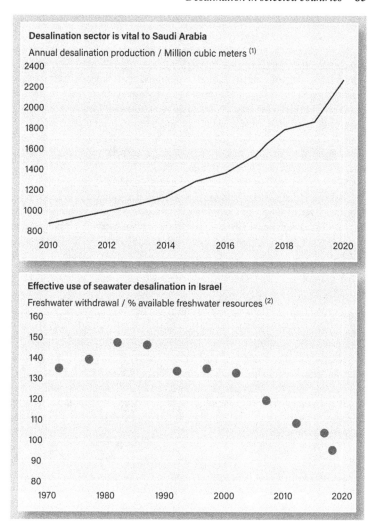

Figure 5.1 Desalination in the Middle East

Sources: (1), Statistics from www.statista.com and Water in Saudi Arabia: Desalination, Wastewater, and Privatisation, US-Saudi Business Council, 2021; (2), World Development Indicators, The World Bank, Update 2022.

(MED). Of the total desalinated water currently produced, 77.5% is produced by MSF, 20.5% by RO, and just 2% by MED plants.

Water desalination is an energy- and a carbon-intensive activity. A significant number of members of the Global Clean Water Desalination Alliance (GCWDA), including Saudi Arabia, committed to a target of 20% of new desalination plants using clean energy and low-carbon processes by 2025; this target would rise to 40% by 2035 and 80% of all new plants after this date. Despite its huge renewable potential, progress towards these targets has been slow, but the country is in a good position to move to another level in terms of renewables deployment because it has the huge financial resources and ready access to the technical capability to do so.

Saudi Arabia has four facilities in the world's ten largest desalination plant list, with its Ras Al Khair plant, or perhaps more accurately, the site, being the largest at over 1 million m^3 per day; Ras Al Khair is a hybrid site utilising both MSF and RO technology. Two of the other three plants use RO technology, and the final plant, an integrated power and water facility, uses MED technology.

5.2.2   Israel

Israel has a growing population and one of the lowest renewable water resources per capita in the world. Agriculture and the domestic sector dominate water consumption. The country has developed its desalination sector significantly since the early 2000s, to the extent that it can export its knowledge and experience to other countries. The sector has five main plants in operation with an annual combined capacity of almost 600 million m^3; a sixth plant will be operating by 2025 and add a further 100 million m^3 per annum. The industry has deployed RO technology with seawater feed, and the electricity consumed is derived, in the main, from fossil generation and from a small but growing renewables sector.

Context for desalination

Israel had a relatively modest population of 9.4 million people in 2021, but it is one of the most densely populated countries in the Middle East at 425 people per km^2, second only to Lebanon but well above other neighbouring countries such as Jordan, Syria, and Egypt. The population has risen by over a factor of four since 1960 and is set to continue to rise, with the growth rate currently running at an average of 1.5% per year. Over 90% of the people live in urban areas, a figure reached in 1980, with the largest city, Jerusalem, the home of just under 10% of the population. In terms of CRI, Israel ranked 128th in the world for 2019, slightly worse than its ranking of 136th over the period 2000–2019.

In terms of fossil fuels, Israel has gas fields off its Mediterranean coast. The volume produced has risen steadily over the last 20 years, with 11.7 billion m^3

in 2021; this is the lowest of all gas producers in the Middle East region, but the reserves-to-production ratio is a healthy 37 years. Israel is currently the largest producer of renewable energy in the region at 5.7 TWh in 2021, delivered through a major deployment of solar energy; this is just under 8% of the country's electricity generation. Looking ahead, Israel has set a target of 40% of electricity generation by renewables by 2030; this would require the deployment of between 18 GW and 23 GW of solar projects, along with 5.5 GW of storage capacity.

Israel's GDP was $489 billion in 2021, and this translates to a GDP per capita of $51.4K, which is in the top 20 economies in the world for this metric. The three major contributors to the GDP were public administration (at 33%), manufacturing (at 26%), and services (21%); contributions to the remaining 20% were from construction (at 11%), transport (at 5%), utilities (at 3%), and agriculture (at 2%). Israel's has a HDI of 0.919, well within the 'very high' human development category, and is ranked 22nd in the world.

Water resources and demand

Israel has one of the lowest renewable water resources per capita in the world at just 84 m^3, while the demand for water resources is double this at 158 m^3 per capita. Freshwater withdrawals to service the needs of a growing population and the economy were running at unsustainable levels in terms of renewable freshwater supplies for several decades. An ambitious growth in its desalination capacity was begun around the turn of this century, and its success has eased the pressure on its natural sources enormously. From 2015 to date, the desalination plant fleet delivered 585 million m^3 each year; assuming a population of 8.5 million in 2019, this equates to 69 m^3 per capita, close to the water extractions from renewable sources.

Recycling of wastewater, primarily for agriculture use, also plays a major role in water management; indeed, Israel's efforts in this area, which required extensive new infrastructure, place the country as the best in the world for this activity. There has also been a major effort to conserve water through education and the application of new technology. Collectively, the desalination programme, recycling of wastewater, and conservation measures mean Israel is now self-sufficient in water supply, and withdrawals of renewable freshwater are sustainable.

Just over 54% of water withdrawals is used to service the needs of the agriculture sector and about 43% for the domestic sector; industry consumes just 3% of annual withdrawals.

Desalination in Israel

Israel was relatively late in the large-scale deployment of desalination technology, but there was recognition in the early 2000s that a growing population and thriving economy, coupled with unsustainable use of its renewable fresh-water supply, needed a radical, technology-led solution. Desalination at scale has proved to be the answer.

The country benefited from a relatively late entry into this sector, thereby adopting the very best technology available at that time and gaining valuable learning as it scaled up its capacity. Its new build programme began with Ashkelon, a 118 million m³ per annum production capacity plant in 2005; two plants quickly followed, Palmachim in 2007 and Hadera in 2009, with an annual capacity of 90 and 127 million m³ per annum, respectively. Two further plants were constructed, Sorek and Ashdod, the former with a 150 million m³ per annum capacity and the latter with a 100 million m³ per annum capacity. All together, these five plants have a production capacity of 585 million m³ per annum.

The sixth desalination plant is under construction: Sorek B will have a 200 million m³ per annum capacity, the tenth largest in the world, and is due to start production in 2023. A seventh plant is also in the final stages of the procurement process; Galilee will have a capacity of 100 million m³ per annum and is expected to begin production in 2025.

Israel chose RO technology, the most energy-efficient of the mainstream technologies available. All the major plants use seawater resources; however, other, smaller plants use 'brackish' feed water. For example, Sabha C desalinates a mixture of seawater and the brine that is discharged from 'brackish' water desalination plants; overall, this results in a more efficient and lower-cost process.

Desalinating water is an electricity-intensive activity. Assuming a total capacity of 585 million m³ per annum and an average electricity use of 4 kWh per m³ for RO technology results in an annual consumption of 2.3 TWh, or 3% of the total generation in Israel. A mix of gas, coal, and solar are used to generate electricity in the country. Gas generation is the largest contributor, with over 61% of the total in 2020; coal generation also makes a significant contribution, with over 27% of the total. At just under 6% in 2020, solar contributes a small but fast-growing contribution to the generation mix. As indicated above, this technology is expected to deliver considerably more in the future at the expense of coal generation, which has already seen a sharp decline over the last 20 years or so, resulting in a lower carbon intensity of production than in the past.

5.2.3 Morocco

Morocco is relatively well placed in terms of renewable water resources, and the level of water stress has remained reasonably stable over the last 40 years. Agriculture uses almost 88% of the total freshwater consumed, while the domestic sector, despite a significant increase in population since 1960, accounts for just 10% of the total. The desalination industry in Morocco is typified by relatively small plants that use brackish feed water. Looking ahead, the government plans to increase desalination capacity enormously following an extended period of drought conditions. It has incentivised the construction of the largest seawater RO plant in Morocco, and in Africa.

Context for desalination

Morocco, like many countries in North Africa and the Middle East, has seen a rapid rise in population over the last 60 years or so; the population in 2021 was 37.1 million, about three times the number in 1960. Nearly 63% of the population in 2022 lived in urban centres, but a significant minority, just over 37%, continued to live in rural areas. The population density is currently at 84 inhabitants per km² which is not high when compared to other similar countries, but the population continues to grow at 1.1% per annum. Morocco ranked 90th out of 182 countries in the CRI for 2019, which is slightly worse than its ranking of 106th for the period 2000–2019.

Unlike other North African countries such as Algeria, Libya, and Egypt, Morocco has low quantities of indigenous fossil resources, and this is in the form of coal. Fossil fuel generation dominated electricity production of 38.5 TWh in 2020, 54% of which was coal, 11% gas, and 10% oil; renewable generation continues to grow, with wind leading the way at 12% and solar at 4%. Morocco has considerable wind and solar potential, and the expectations are that these will displace fossil fuels in the power sector in the future. There has also been hydroelectricity in the country since the early 1960s, and generation amounted to 2.3% of the total in 2020, but the annual output varies considerably from one year to the next, from a low of 0.7 TWh and a high of 3.5 TWh over the last 20 years or so to an average of 1.5 TWh over this period.

The GDP of Morocco in 2021 was $143 billion, and this translates to a very low GDP per capita value of just over $3.5K, despite a steady rise over recent decades. Services contributed 51% of GDP in 2020, followed by industry with 26% and agriculture with 12%. GDP growth has fluctuated over the years, but in the three years pre-COVID, the economy grew by 4.3%, 3.2%, and 2.7%. Agriculture remains a very important sector and employs 33% of the population; 44% of the population work in services and 23% in industry. Morocco has a HDI of 0.683, which is within the 'medium' human development category and is ranked 123rd in the world. All these indicators are typical of a developing country.

Water resources and demand

For its size of population and its current development, Morocco is reasonably well placed in terms of renewable water resources; its annual freshwater withdrawals in 2021 amount to just under 37% of the total internal resources. This masks significant regional differences in the country, and limited technical and economic capability and leaky infrastructure cannot compensate for these differences.

Unconventional water resources contribute to the water supply to help alleviate overuse of natural resources. Desalination of both seawater and brackish water and recycling of wastewater all contribute to supply. Morocco has 3,500 km of coastal potential and an estimated 500 million m^3 of brackish water. Groundwater quality can be poor due to high evaporation and low recharge; there is also intrusion by seawater, the leakage of nitrates, fertilisers, and pesticides from agriculture, and a lack of wastewater treatment.

Looking ahead, the Moroccan government plans to invest heavily in wastewater treatment facilities to increase the volume treated from 70 million m^3 to 1 billion m^3 with the water used for agriculture; such treatment plants will also be constructed near industrial areas.

The agriculture sector dominates freshwater water consumption, using almost 88% of the total, with the domestic sector a distant second at 10% of the total; industry uses just 2% of the total. Tourism is an important sector for the country, contributing about 7% to GDP and is a significant employer, but tourism is heavily reliant on a reliable supply of pure water, and its provision is a challenge for the country.

Desalination in Morocco

Morocco began the deployment of desalination technology with two very small plants in the 1970s, one using seawater and the other using brackish water; by 2019, the sector had plants helping to service the needs of nine cities with a total capacity of 120,000 m^3 per day, or 44 million m^3 each year. Many of the plants are on a small scale, the maximum being a few tens of thousands production capacity. Unlike many other countries with a long coast and easy access to the sea, most of the desalination capacity to date in Morocco uses brackish water; in fact, brackish water desalination capacity was three times the conventional seawater type in 2019.

However, this is about to change. Following several years of drought conditions, the government decided it needed to increase its desalination capacity significantly and incentivised the construction of by far the largest seawater desalination plant in Morocco, near Agadir; it is also the largest desalination plant in Africa. This project is a public-private enterprise, with the government providing over $400 million for the project. The private company that won the contract will construct and manage the entire plant for the next 27 years.

This new plant, which began operating in 2022, uses RO technology to produce 275,000 m^3 of desalinated water per day, of which 125,000 is reserved for irrigation to relieve pressure on the local groundwater resources; there are plans to increase capacity of this plant to 450,000 m^3 per day. This project will include all the infrastructure needed to realise its full potential, including reservoirs for storing drinking water, five pumping stations, over 20 km of pipelines, and about 500 km of distribution network.

There is an expectation that the water crisis will continue, not least because the many dams in the country are not being replenished to the same levels as in the past, and a belief that climate change will make the situation worse. In response to the deteriorating situation, the government has announced plans to have 20 desalination plants operating over the next decade or so, up from the nine plants today. The idea is that such plants can provide potable water to meet the needs of its cities, releasing water from its dams to service the needs of inner regions. Also, the government has signalled that it wishes to exploit its large renewable energy potential to help meet the energy needs of its desalination plants.

5.2.4 Spain

Spain suffers from drought conditions for varying periods of time, sometimes intense and sometimes less so. Its renewable water per capita value is very much lower than the global average, and the water stress level remains high. Agriculture consumes almost two-thirds of the water withdrawals, with industry and the domestic sector dividing the rest. Spain has a highly successful and mature desalination sector with 765 plants of varying capacity. The plants use both seawater and brackish water in almost equal measure, and the preferred technology is now RO. Spain exports its knowledge and expertise in desalination around the world.

Context for desalination

The population of Spain has grown from just under 34 million in 1970 to 47 million in 2010, an increase of just under 40%, and then stabilised at that number in the following decade to 2020. It is the 7th largest country by population and the 4th largest by land area (500 km^2) in Europe, if Russia and Turkey are included, both of which are larger in both measures. Its population density is 95 inhabitants per km^2, which is in the middle of the selected case study countries.

The economy has grown rapidly, with average GDP growth of just under 3% in recent years. Despite this healthy growth, Spain's GDP in 2021 was $1,427 billion and its GDP per capita was just $30K, ranking 18th in a Europe of 46 countries. Services dominate the economy with a contribution of 74.5% of GDP in 2019 followed by industry at 22.6% and agriculture at just 2.9%; employment statistics by sector follow the GDP contributions. Spain has a HDI of 0.905, well within the 'very high' human development category and is the 27th ranked country in the world.

Spain imports about 75% of its energy, with coal reserves, its only indigenous fossil fuel. This dependency has driven a large deployment of renewables to the extent that this sector now dominates electricity generation with 95 TWh or 35% of the total in 2021; wind generation amounted to just over 62 TWh while solar contributed almost 27 TWh. The next largest contributor to electricity generation was gas at 69 TWh or 25% of the total, followed by nuclear at 57 TWh or 21%; hydroelectricity is also an important contributor, with just under 30 TWh or 11% of the total generation.

Renewables, then, play an important role in Spain's electricity supply, but a limitation is the absence of large-scale storage, which would help address the inherent intermittency of these technologies. Other technologies play an important role: nuclear with its baseload generation and gas, which can provide generation when needed; hydroelectricity also provides much needed flexibility to the system.

In terms of its CRI, Spain ranked 32nd out of 182 countries in 2019, the same level of vulnerability as that over the period 2000–2019. The country has suffered regular episodes of drought over the last 50 years. There have been four short, intense droughts and three prolonged drought episodes in this period; these, and a rapidly growing population, prompted the government to manage its renewable water resources well and to encourage the development of a thriving desalination industry.

Water resources and demand

Water stress in Spain is currently at just under 43%, down from the high of 60% in the late 1980s. Total freshwater withdrawals are 31 billion m^3 and represent 28.1% of internal resources in Spain in 2022; the country has an overall 2,376 m^3 freshwater per capita value. However, this masks the fact that Spain, like many countries that circle the Mediterranean, is a dry country and one of the most water-stressed developed countries.

As occurs in many countries, water withdrawals for agriculture take the lion's share of the water used, amounting to 65% of the total in 2018; industry is the second largest consumer at 19% of the total, while the domestic sector consumes just under 16%. The average daily water consumption by inhabitants in Spain was 132 litres in 2018, down from a peak value of 171 litres in the early 2000s. As indicated earlier, the population has plateaued at around 47 million over the period 2010–2020; this means a total water consumption of about 6 million m^3 per day.

Water resources also include water from desalination plants. Collectively, the plants have a total capacity of 5 million m^3 per day, or 1.8 billion m^3 each year. This can be compared to the total freshwater withdrawals, plus desalination, of 31 billion m^3 per year. Desalination, then, contributes almost 6% to Spain's total freshwater withdrawals; it also represents over 80% of the daily water consumed by its inhabitants.

Desalination in Spain

This is a highly successful industry in Spain, which began with the first desalination plant in Europe installed in Lanzarote in the Canary Islands in 1964. As indicated earlier, the country now has 765 plants of various sizes, ranging

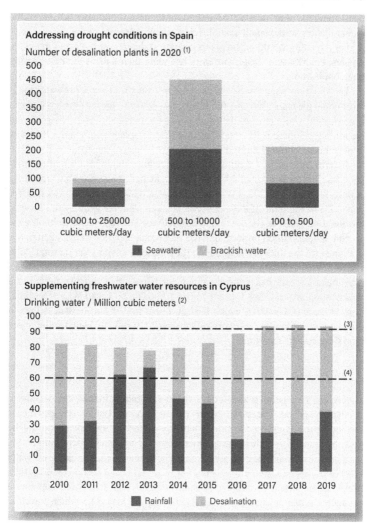

Figure 5.2 Desalination in the Europe

Source: (1), Spanish desalination know-how, a world-wide benchmark, Laura F Zraza, Smart Water Magazine, 2022; (2), Cyprus Water Development Department, www.moa.gov.cy.

Notes: (3), Maximum potential quantity of water delivered by five desalination plants with a total capacity of 237 000 cubic meters per day; (4), Contracted volume in 2022.

from hundreds of m³ per day to hundreds of thousands of m³ per day. Over 200 plants operate at the small-scale level, while 450 operate in the thousands of m³ per day; almost 100 of the plants operate at the largest scale and make the greatest contribution. Spain currently has more than half of the desalination plants in Europe.

Desalination plants in Spain use both seawater and brackish water in almost equal measure: 360 and 405 plants, respectively; most of the large plants use seawater while most of the small plants use brackish water. The preferred technology adopted is RO, and there are several Spanish companies that now export this technology around the world.

In terms of energy, 1.8 billion m³ would require about 7.3 TWh of electricity, assuming an average of 4 kWh/m³. As indicated above, the total electricity supply in 2021 was 272 TWh, with the desalination sector accounting for just 2.7% of the total. If the electricity is taken from the grid, then a third of the electricity needed for desalination is delivered by renewable technologies.

Small desalination projects that use renewable electricity have been in operation since the mid-1990s in Spain; these have involved solar thermal, solar PV, and wind generation. The dramatic decline in costs of these technologies over the last decade has reduced a significant barrier to their deployment in the desalination process. Spain is a member of the Global Clean Water Desalination Alliance (GCWDA), which has set a goal for 20% of new desalination plants to be powered by renewables between 2020 and 2025 and further, more ambitious targets thereafter.

5.2.5 Cyprus

Cyprus is a very popular tourist destination, particularly in the more developed south of the island. The growth of this industry over the last few decades means the population of almost one million inhabitants 'flexes' dramatically during the year, by as much as 50% in the summer months. The island suffers from highly variable rainfall and, despite all the rivers being dammed to create freshwater reservoirs, there is severe over-stressing of groundwater resources. Desalination is an important contributor to water security, with five plants capable of producing a nameplate capacity of 235,000 m³ per day. The Water Development Department contracts with the utilities that operate the plants for the water it believes it will need, considering factors such as demand projections, available internal freshwater resources, and price; this means that the desalination plants may not be working at their maximum nameplate production all the time.

Context for desalination

Cyprus is the third largest island in the Mediterranean with a land area of 9,250 km² and is situated at the eastern end of the sea; at its longest, it is 225 km east-to-west, and at its widest, it is 97 km north-to-south. Politically and ethnically, the island is separated into two geographical areas, with the largest in the south of the island occupying about 5,750 km², while the north occupies about 3,500 km². There are interactions between the two regions; for example, the community in the south supplies electricity to the north, and the use of renewable water resources in one community effects the other. There are also two sizeable sovereign British military bases on the south coast of the island.

The total population is over 1.2 million, about three-quarters of which reside in the south. Tourism is a major sector for the island, with almost 2 million visitors in 2021, about half the peak number visiting the island in 2019 before the COVID pandemic. The number of visitors is now rising again, and the government needs to plan its energy, water, and food needs for numbers of visitors like those in the pre-pandemic period.

This small island state had a GDP of $28 billion dollars in 2021, a healthy GDP growth of 2.6%, and a GDP per capita value of almost $31K. Sector contributions to GDP have remained very similar over the last ten years, with the services sector dominating at about 75%, with industry, including manufacturing, contributing about 20%, and agriculture contributing about 2%. Cyprus has a HDI of 0.896 and is ranked 29th in the world.

Cyprus had little in the way of indigenous fossil fuel resources, but offshore exploration in recent years has found significant gas fields which are expected to start producing in the mid-2020s. The country imports fossil fuels, in part to produce electricity in its thermal plants. Total electricity production has remained steady over the last 20 years at about 5.0 TWh, a remarkable achievement when the population has grown by almost 30% and the tourism industry grew significantly to a pre-COVID peak of almost 4 million visitors per year. Renewable generation has also grown over the last decade or so and amounted to 0.8 TWh in 2021; this was made up of 0.5 TWh solar, 0.2 TWh wind, and 0.1 TWh biomass.

Water resources and demand

Cyprus has a significant mountain range in the form of the Troodos mountains, and this plays an important role in the water resources on the island, both north and south of the dividing line between the two communities. All the rivers have dams to create freshwater reservoirs. Water stress has varied markedly over the last 50 years or so, from a low of 20% in 1977 to a high of 35% in 2012; in 2018, the water stress indicator was 28%. It is recognised as the most water-stressed country in the European Union.

It is important that freshwater demand can be met sustainably through rainfall, desalination, and recycled water, but over the last decade, there have been years when this has not been the case. Against an average annual demand of about 260 million m³ in the period 2010–2019, the sum of these three sources of water was just 145 million m³ in 2013 and a plentiful 455 million m³ in 2019; the main reason for this is the highly variable contribution by rainfall. Not surprisingly, there is evidence that Cyprus is severely over-stressing its groundwater resources, even with the government introducing measures to curtail water use during periods of low rainfall. The island had a CRI ranking of 130 in the world in 2019, which is slightly worse than its average Index for the period 2000–2019.

The agricultural sector was 59% of the total water demand in 2020, higher than the 35% needed for the municipal sector and much higher than the 6% used by industry. The tourist industry is now a very important sector for the country, bringing huge benefits to the economy.

Desalination in Cyprus

Desalination has played an increasingly important role in the provision of water for the island over the last 25 years. Five plants are now in operation, all in the south of the island: three at 60,000 m³/day, one at 40,000 m³ per day and the latest at just 15,000 m³ per day; the total maximum capacity, then, is 235 K m³/day or 86.5 million m³ per year. Crucially, the five desalination plants have the technical capacity to meet all the drinking water needs of the population, network infrastructure permitting. In practice, some of the drinking water needs are met by reservoirs replenished in the winter months, and once the levels are established, the government contracts the capacity it needs to make up any potential shortfall from the desalination plants.

The total cost of desalinated water in 2022 was estimated to be just under €90 million (or just under $100) for 53 million m³, or 54% of the water consumed (this production is much lower than the maximum design production capacity highlighted above). The total cost includes a fee for water not produced because the Water Development Department also contracts to pay the cost of providing reserves. The cost of water varies by plant: the lowest production cost is €1.04 per m³ (or about $1.1 per m³) with a cost of €0.07 per m³ (or $0.08 per m³) for providing reserve; the highest production cost is €1.74 per m³ (or $1.9 per m³) and if placed in the reserve, €0.36 per m³ (or $0.04 per m³).

There are many smaller desalination units being used to meet more local needs: by municipalities for drinking water, by power stations and industry, and by tourist facilities. The capacity of these small-scale plants ranges from 54 m³ per day to 2,400 m³ per day.

All the main desalination plants use RO technology and exploit seawater resources. The electricity needed to deliver the maximum capacity is 0.35 TWh, or 7% of the total electricity consumed on the island.

5.2.6   *United Kingdom*

The UK was an average 0.2°C warmer over the last 15 years compared to the previous 15 years. The last 30 years have seen some unusually hot, dry summers, particularly in the south of the country, and a new UK record temperature of 40.3°C was set on the 19 July 2022. The domestic sector accounts for almost 75% of the water consumed. The country has one desalination plant built as a contingency for use in periods of long dry spells. It began operation in 2010 with RO technology and is located on the Thames estuary, where freshwater and saline water mix. A second major plant has been abandoned, in part following local opposition.

Context for desalination

The United Kingdom (UK) had the 21st largest population in the world in 2021, with over 67 million inhabitants. The population has risen over 30% since 1950 and is projected to grow a further 13% by 2050. Its population density at 280 people/km^2 is higher than that of its European neighbours with similar populations, such as Germany, Italy, and France, and very much higher than that of Spain and Poland. In one sense, the UK benefited economically from being at the forefront of the industrial revolution in the 19th century by putting in place an extensive water (and energy) infrastructure; in another sense, despite continual renewal, some of the infrastructure is old and not necessarily in the right place to meet the needs of a burgeoning population and changing climate. The HDI ranking for the UK was 0.929, placing it 19th in the world.

The UK was the 5th largest economy in the world in 2021 with a GDP of just over $3,100 billion and a GDP per capita of about $47,300. Services made the largest contribution to the economy, with just over 79% of GDP, followed by industry at 20% and agriculture at under 1%; this distribution is typical of most developed countries.

The ready availability of coal resources underpinned the UK's industrial revolution and transformed its economy and society in the 19th century and most of the 20th. The North Sea has also provided the UK with access to considerable oil and gas resources in the second half of the last century, and this has continued to date. It benefited hugely in terms of energy security and provided considerable tax revenues for the government to further the wellbeing of its citizens.

Electricity supply was once dominated by coal and, to a lesser extent, nuclear generation. This has changed dramatically over the last few decades, first with gas generation in the 1990s and then the deployment of the various renewable technologies: wind, biomass, and solar photovoltaic. In 2021, a total supply of 310 TWh was dominated by gas and renewables generation at 124 TWh and 117 TWh, respectively; nuclear also made a valuable contribution of 46 TWh, with hydroelectricity, coal, and oil generation making very small contributions to the total. The carbon intensity of the mix has fallen dramatically over the last 30 years, and this decline must continue if the UK is to meet its climate change targets over the period to 2050.

The UK's geographical position off the European continent means its weather is moderated by the Gulf Stream, so it enjoys mild and wet weather.

The mean annual temperature for the UK over the last 30 years or so has ranged from a low of 8°C to a high of 9.6°C; overall, the average for the second half of this 30-year period was 0.2°C higher than the first 15 years. This period has had some unusually hot, dry summers, with those in 1995, 2018, and 2022 particularly so; a new UK record temperature of 40.3°C was set on the 19 July 2022. The UK had a CRI ranking of 102 out of 182 countries in 2019, which is a considerable improvement on its ranking of 58 for the period 2000–2019.

Rising temperature is consistent with climate change model predictions from the UK. For example, rainfall patterns are changing, with a drier southern part of the UK and a wetter north. Also predicted are heavier showers, which deliver large volumes of water in relatively short periods. The result can be flooding, in part because the existing and ageing infrastructure cannot cope with the increased flow of water; unfortunately, this also means that valuable water resources are lost, particularly in the south-east of the country where it is needed.

Water resources and demand

At the macro level, water indicators for the UK remain good; for example, annual freshwater withdrawals as a percentage of internal resources are less than 6%, while renewable water resources per capita are over 2,000 m³. Overall, water stress levels have improved over the last 30 years, from over 20% in the 1990s to less than 15% in recent years. However, these statistics mask regional differences, with the north better endowed with water resources than the south; climate change is starting to exacerbate these differences, and the infrastructure has not yet evolved to accommodate the changes expected in the future.

Unlike most other countries, water demand is dominated by the UK domestic sector, which consumes about 74% of the total 8.4 billion m³ per year; industry and agriculture share the remaining 26%. The largest city and capital is London is in the south-east of the country and has a major river, the Thames, going through it. Although not on the scale of some of the megacities in the world, its population was 9 million in 2020, having grown by over 30% since 1990. Assuming a daily water consumption of 150 litres per capita per day, London had a water demand of 1.35 million m³ per day in 2020.

Desalination in the UK

The UK has one major desalination plant on the banks of the Thames River and a small plant on the island of Jersey. Most people in the UK are unaware that the UK has a desalination plant, even in the south-east of England where the plant is located. The Gateway (previously known as the Becton) Thames Desalination plant, is a state-of-the-art RO plant with a design capacity of 150,000 m³ per day; the capacity was downrated to 100,000 m³ per day in 2022. It began operation in 2010 and was designed to provide drinking water when London and other parts of the south-east of England had drought conditions; it was an important contingency measure for the 2012 London Olympics. It can also be used to provide water for reservoirs that serve London and the surrounding area. When needed, this plant can supply about 7% of the total water needs of London.

Gateway is an energy efficient plant, in part because the water is 'brackish' at that location with fresh river water mixed with seawater; the energy used is further minimised by exploiting the tide of the river and the adoption of various energy efficiency measures, including Pelton turbines and variable speed turbines. It must also accommodate the water salinity that changes through the seasons. The average power consumption was estimated at 14 MW, which results in an energy usage of 2.27 kWh per m³ of water produced.

Jersey is the largest of the English Channel's islands and is home to almost 110,000 people. It has had a desalination plant since 1970, the first of which was a MSF distillation process, subsequently replaced by a RO plant in 1999 with a capacity of 6,000 m³ per day. In 2016, the plant capacity was increased to almost 11,000 m³ per day, which is about half of the island's daily demand for water.

Model projections suggest that climate change will lead to more drought conditions in the south of the UK; these conditions and a rising population over the next few decades will lead to greater pressure on water resources. There is an expectation that more desalination plants will be needed in the future, but one major project that was planned on the south coast of England has been abandoned because of local opposition.

5.2.7   United States of America

Overall, the United States of America (USA) would appear to be well endowed with water resources, but this disguises water stress at the state level in the south and west of the country. Here, rainfall is low, and water abstraction from groundwater sources can be at unsustainable levels. Desalination is being used to help provide water security in 35 states, with three states – Florida, California, and Texas – accounting for almost 70% of the 400 or so plants. The dominant technology is RO using brackish water, with over 70% of the plants using this combination.

Context for desalination

The USA is the world's 3rd largest country, with a land area of over 9.8 million km² and the 3rd largest country by population, with about 332 million inhabitants in 2021. The country is made up of 50 states, each with its own distinctive characteristics; for example, Alaska is geographically the largest state with almost 18% of the land area, while the most populous is California with over 39 million people. Most of the states have a coastal border, including seven bordering the Great Lakes.

The country boasts the world's largest economy at over $23 trillion, followed by China at almost $18 trillion, with all other countries far behind; it also enjoys a very high GDP per capita value of just over $69,000. Overall, services make by far the largest contribution to GDP, accounting for over 81% of the total in 2021, while industry contributes 18% and agriculture just under 1%. The HDI for the USA is 0.921, which places the country 21st in the world.

The USA was the 2nd largest consumer of primary energy and the 2nd largest emitter of CO_2 in 2021 after China. The country is rich in fossil and renewable resources and ranks 1st in gas generation in the world, 3rd in coal, 1st in nuclear, 4th in hydroelectricity, and 2nd in renewables. Energy-related metrics vary significantly across the states; for example, in terms of electricity supply, the state with the largest coal generation is West Virginia; the largest in terms of gas generation is Delaware; for hydroelectricity, it is Washington; for nuclear, it is New Hampshire; for solar, it is California; and for wind, it is South Dakota.

Electricity generation has grown by over a third since 1990 to 4,400 TWh in 2021. Gas and renewables generation has displaced coal, resulting in the carbon intensity falling, a process that has occurred in many other developed countries.

Water resources and demand

Industry and agriculture used most water resources in 2017, with 47% and 40% of the total, respectively, while the domestic sector accounted for about 13%. Total freshwater withdrawals amounted to about 440 billion m³ in 2017, or almost 1,370 m³ per capita, assuming a population of 325 million in that year. The latter compares well with the 8,620 m³ per capita of available renewable freshwater resources, although this number is just over half of the global average.

Overall, then, the USA is relatively well endowed with water resources, with freshwater withdrawals amounting to less than 16% of the total internal resources in 2018. Water stress has improved slightly, from 32% in the 1980s to 28% in the last decade. But these metrics can be misleading with major regional differences; for example, rainfall in Louisiana is over 150 cm a year while Nevada gets less than 25 cm. In some regions, there is a reduction in freshwater flow into the basins that channel rain and snow into the rivers that service the needs of communities.

Aquifers are also being exploited, with about half the population relying on the groundwater contained in these ancient reservoirs for drinking water; it is also being exploited for agriculture and for the manufacturing industry. Water from these reservoirs is being pumped out faster than it can be replenished.

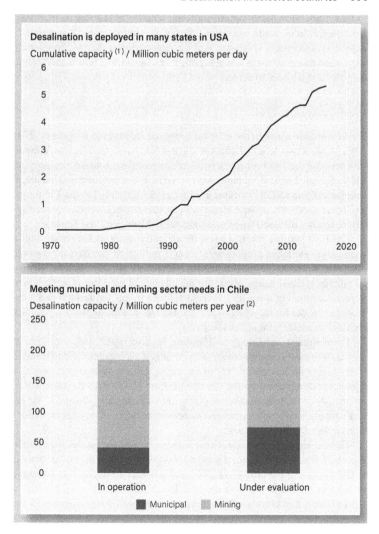

Figure 5.3 Desalination in North and South America

Sources: (1), Adapted from Updated and Extended Survey of U.S. Municipal Desalination Plant, U.S. Department of the Interior Bureau of Reclamation, 2018; (2), Current situation and Challenges of desalination in Chile, Sebastian Herrera-Leon, Desalination and Water Treatment, Volume 171, p93, 2019.

The USA, then, faces significant water challenges in some of its States, most notably in the south and west of the country. Indeed, some States already experience freshwater shortages, and the expectation is that with a growing population and decreasing water supply, many others will follow this path in the years and decades to come.

Desalination in the USA

The desalination sector in the USA has grown considerably in the period 1970–2017. The first two decades had a low single-figure build rate; this was followed by a period in the 1990s when the build rate increased to about 6 plants per year, and then about double this number more recently. There were over 400 municipal desalination plants in 2017 located in 35 States; three States - Florida, California, and Texas – had 68% of these plants, with another 5 States collectively accounting for another 16%, and the remaining states had between 1 and 8 plants.

The USA has the fourth largest desalination sector in the world with a cumulative municipal production of over 5 million m³ per day; the average plant size, however, is small at less than 15,000 m³ per day capacity. Almost all municipal desalination plants are inland and are used for water treatment to produce drinking water and, to a much lesser extent, wastewater treatment producing water for recycling; a few are used for producing water for aquifer recharge or aquifer storage and recovery.

The dominant technology is RO using brackish water with over 72% of the plants using this combination; the next largest contributor is Nanofiltration technology with just under 14% of the plants. Unlike other countries with a significant desalination sector, the combination of RO with seawater makes up just 3% of the total number of plants although this may change in the future with elevated temperatures and increased incidence of drought conditions expected under climate change.

The top ten largest desalination plants are in just four states: California, Florida, Texas, and Arizona. At almost 190,000 m³ per day, the largest plant is in California and uses RO technology and seawater feed; this is comparable to some of the major plants in the Middle East. Seven of the top ten largest USA plants are in Florida, one in Texas, and one in Arizona. Together, these ten plants have a combined capacity of over 1 million m³ per day, which is 20% of the USA total municipal capacity.

5.2.8   Chile

Chile is in the top 25 in the world in terms of the CRI. Overall, there are plentiful freshwater resources in Chile, but these are not always where they are needed. The northern regions are highly water-stressed while the southern regions have plentiful supplies of freshwater. One of the country's key exports, copper, is mined in the northern regions and uses freshwater in the extraction process; the answer to this need has been desalination. This technology has been used in Chile for over a century, for mining and to service the domestic sector. There has been significant growth over the last two decades, with RO and seawater feed being the dominant technologies deployed.

Context for desalination

Chile is the longest and narrowest country in the world. It is flanked on one side by the Andes Mountains and the other by the Pacific Ocean. It is a country of contrasts, containing the driest desert in the world and is home to ancient glaciers. Its population was 19.5 million people in 2021, with an annual growth rate of just 0.1%.

Its economy is small, at $317 billion, with a GDP per capita value of just under $16,500 in 2021. Services contribute most to GDP at just under 63%, followed by industrial production at just under 34%; agriculture contributes less than 4%. Mining is a key industry for the country, with copper being the major export, amounting to about $33 billion, or almost half the country's total exports in 2019. Chile's HDI is 0.855 and ranks 42 in the world.

Electricity production in Chile has contributions from all the major technologies. Fossil generation makes up almost 50% of the total of 88 TWh in 2021, the remainder being made up of low-carbon generation in the form of hydroelectricity (19%), wind (11%), solar (12%), and geothermal and biomass (9.5%). The growth in electricity supply over the last decade of 18 TWh has been met by a combination of the new renewables of solar and wind; in contrast, hydro and fossil fuel generation have remained broadly static.

Chile's CRI ranking has declined markedly in the last two decades, making it more vulnerable to extreme weather events. It was ranked 25th out of a total of 182 countries in 2019, compared to a ranking of 83 over the last two decades.

Water resources and demand

Chile has one of the highest renewable water resources in the world, at just over 47,000 m^3 per capita, and one of the lowest annual freshwater withdrawals, at 4.0% of internal resources. Nonetheless, water stress – the *freshwater withdrawal as a proportion of available freshwater resources* – has grown significantly over the last 20 years, from 5% in the early 1990s to over 22% in 2018.

There are major differences in water demand and supply in the 15 regions that span the length of the country. Demand outstrips supply in the six northern regions and in two of these regions by a significant margin. The regions in the south benefit from supply being more than demand, and the further south, the greater the excess supply.

Agriculture is the largest consumer of freshwater, amounting to 83% of the total, with industry using 13% and the domestic sector under 4%. Mining is an important industry for the country, and as indicated earlier, copper mining is a valuable export. This activity is carried out in the northern, drier regions of the country, and since copper mining is a water-intensive activity, the industry must find sustainable solutions, and desalination is now a very important supplier of water for this industry.

Desalination in Chile

As in many countries, desalination has been used in Chile since the late 19th century, but the industry has seen significant growth in the last decade or two. There were 11 desalination plants in operation in 2018 above a threshold of 1,000 m³ per day, all in the northern third of the country; three of these were for municipal use and the remaining eight to service the water needs of the industrial sector, mostly copper mining but also one steel plant. The total capacity of the plants amounts to just over 0.5 million m³ per day of which 77% was used in the industrial sector and just 23% for municipal use. Both the largest and the smallest desalination plants are found in copper mining, the former producing over 200,000 m³ per day and the latter just over 3,000 m³ per day.

Not surprisingly, with such a long coastline, the dominant technology is RO with seawater feed (RO-SW); there is just one operational plant that treats river water for municipal purposes. One problem associated with RO-SW in Chile is the need to transport the seawater feed and brine waste long distances to the mines in the mountains, perhaps 1,000 metres above sea level, via pipelines. Seawater is corrosive, so high-quality materials for the pipes and equipment are needed, and considerable energy is consumed pumping water long distances.

The average electricity consumption of these plants is typically about 4.5 kWh per m³ which means the desalination industry consumes over 0.8 TWh each year. As noted above, over half the electricity generated in 2021 was from low-carbon sources such as wind and solar, hydroelectricity, geothermal, and biomass.

Looking ahead, a further 10 plants were under evaluation in 2018, 4 for municipal purposes and 6 for the industry sector; collectively, these amount to an additional capacity of 0.6 million m³ per day if all the projects are developed, 35% of which will be for the municipal sector and 65% for the industry sector. However, the mining industry does not require water of the level of purity produced by desalination, and there may be bespoke technical solutions to meet the needs of individual mining environments.

Also, desalinated water may increasingly be needed by the agriculture sector to improve the food security of the country. The desalination industry, then, must consider all the factors of its projects – economic and social, technical, and energy use – as it grows in the future.

5.2.9 China

Water stress in China has risen over the last 40 years, with some regions, particularly in the west and south of the country where most of the population lives, more affected than others. China has a clear plan for the desalination sector in the period to 2025 and an ambition for continued growth beyond that. It is rapidly developing its capability in the sector, following the path it has successfully followed for other sectors such as mining, power, and manufacturing. RO combined with seawater is the dominant technology, but the government is also encouraging the deployment and building up of its capabilities, in other mainstream commercial technologies, such as MSF and MED.

Context for desalination

China is the 4th largest country in the world with a land area of 9.6 million km², almost the same as Canada or the USA, and had the largest population of over 1.4 billion in 2019. It is home to the Gobi Desert, the 3rd largest desert in the world, covering 1.3 million km² and the 10th longest coastline in the world, at 14,500 km; it also has several mountain ranges across the country.

Mainland China is classified into three different geographic regions: eastern, central, and western. Most of the population lives in the eastern and central regions, and the relatively small population living in the western region has lower economic and human development compared to the other regions. The country has four of the largest cities in the world top 20, in terms of population, including Shanghai (3rd largest) and Beijing (9th largest); about 60% of the population lives in urban centres.

The country is now the world's second-largest economy, at almost $18 trillion in 2021; however, the per capita value of GDP, at about $12,600 languishes well behind developed countries. The main contributors to GDP by value in 2019 are services at a relatively low value of almost 54%, industry at a relatively high value of 39%, and agriculture at just over 7%; employment shows a different distribution with 47%, 27%, and 25% for each of these sectors, respectively. The HDI for China is 0.768, placing it in the 'high' category and 78th out of 191 countries in the world.

China was the largest consumer of primary energy and the largest emitter of CO_2 in 2021. Its fossil fuels are dominated by coal, and the country produced over 4,100 million tonnes in 2021, about half of the world total; it also has some indigenous gas production and a little oil production. The country is by far the largest producer of electricity, at about 30% of the world total in 2021. The sector has major contributions from all the low carbon technologies – nuclear, hydroelectricity, and renewables – amounting to about 34% of the total generation.

Water resources and demand

Agriculture was the largest user of freshwater, accounting for over 64%, followed by industry with over 22%; the domestic sector accounted for over 13%. Some key industries, such as the petrochemical sector, steel production, and fossil and nuclear plants, are located on the coast in water-scarce regions, and China is seeking solutions to this growing problem.

Water stress in China has risen from just under 34% in 1982 to around 43% in 2018, the latter being lower than the 70% global average. Freshwater withdrawals amounted to just under 600 billion m^3 in 2017, eclipsing all other countries; annual freshwater withdrawals were 21% of internal resources, while renewable resources were about 2,000 m^3 per capita, considerably lower than the global average of almost 15,000 m^3 per capita.

As with other large countries, some regions in China have less freshwater availability than others. The country's water resources are concentrated in southern China, with the rest of the country experiencing drought conditions; some rivers, lakes, and aquifers have dried up due to over-extraction, and some surface water has been polluted to the extent that it is no longer fit for drinking. A growing demand brought about by population growth, economic activity, urbanisation, and climate change has led to lower availability of freshwater; the concern is that the lack of freshwater is having a detrimental impact on economic development. The CRI for China placed it 32nd in the world in 2019, a deterioration from the ranking of 41st for the period 2000–2019.

The government has brought in a range of measures to improve water supply, including improved water management, efficiency measures, and implementing trans-basin water diversion projects across the country. For example, China has already built several new canals transferring water from the flood-prone Yangtze River to the drought-stricken Yellow River regions of the north, a project known as the South-North Water Diversion Project. Other measures include wastewater recycling, rainwater harvesting, and desalination projects.

Desalination in China

China is a relative newcomer to the desalination industry, but it is following a similar approach it has successfully used in other sectors such as energy: a target is set in China's five-year plans, followed by a willingness to explore a variety of technology options, underpinned by a concerted effort to build the requisite internal technical capability and industrial capacity in the sector.

The result is very encouraging. The country had very few plants in operation at the turn of this century, but two decades later, it has close to 160 plants in the eight regions along its coastline and the island of Hainan. The total nameplate capacity of the fleet is over 1.5 million m^3 per day with two regions – Shandong and Zhejiang – accounting for over 50% of the plants and just under 50% of the total capacity deployed.

As in many parts of the world the dominant technology is RO-SW in China, followed by MED; both technologies have been deployed on the same site in some projects. Three other technologies have been used, albeit, on a much smaller scale: Multi-Stage Flash (MSF) desalination, Electrodialysis (ED), and Forward Osmosis (FO). RO-SW makes up 55% of the total and MED just over

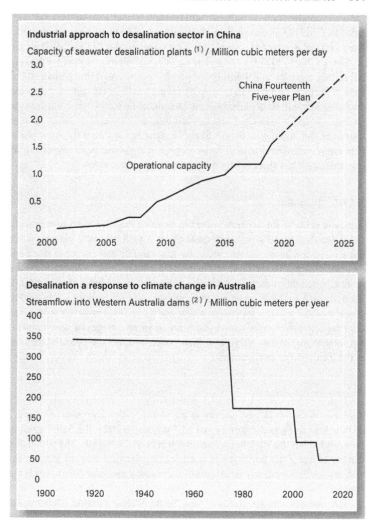

Figure 5.4 Desalination in Asia and Oceania

Sources: (1), Progress and Perspectives of Desalination in China, Guoling Ruan et al., Membranes, Volume 11, p206, 2021; (2), Climate Trends in Western Australia, Department of Primary Industries and Regional Development based on data from Water Corporation of Western Australia, 2020.

26%; the combination of RO and MED adds a further 17% to the total, with MSF, ED, and FO much less than 1% combined. Plant size varies significantly, from a 100 m³ per day ED plant to over 200,000 m³ per day RO and MED plants. China's 2021–2025 five-year plan includes an ambitious target for the sector, raising capacity to 2.9 million m³ per day by the end of the period. About 85% of the new 1.25 million m³ per day capacity will be for coastal cities, and the remainder will be deployed inland. Desalinated water will become a major backup source for municipal supplies and industries in regions suffering from shortages, and more growth will likely be signalled in future five-year plans. It is likely that China will, at some stage in the future, begin exporting its expertise, as it has successfully done so with other industries.

5.2.10   *Australia*

Australia is in the top 20 in the world in terms of the CRI. With its relatively small population and significant resources, it is well placed to meet its water challenges, the latter brought about by low rainfall and extended dry periods. Some of the states, particularly in the south and west of the country, are more affected than others. The desalination sector in Australia has around 270 plants, mostly small in scale, but there are six large plants built since 2006 to improve water security for coastal cities, and these alone make up 60% of the total capacity. New desalination plants are in various stages of development, but some communities are voicing their concerns about the potential damage to the local marine environment.

Context for desalination

Australia is the 7th largest country in the world, with a land area of over 7.7 million km² and a population of just 25.7 million in 2021, the 55th largest in the world; it has the 7th longest coastline at around 29,000 km. The population density is just 3 per km² but this is misleading because most of the population resides in a relatively small part of the country and generally towards the coast.

The country has six states – New South Wales, Victoria, Queensland, Western Australia, South Australia, and the island of Tasmania – and two territories: the Northern Territory and the Australian Capital Territory. Western Australia is the largest with 33% of the land area, while New South Wales is the most populous state, with 32% of the total. Most of the country's population, about 77%, resides in the 15 largest cities, and Sydney and Melbourne between them account for just over 40% of the total population.

Economic activity amounted to almost $1.6 trillion with a GDP per capita value of $60,000, which is in the world's top 20 countries. As with all highly developed countries, services make the largest contribution to the country's GDP at 71%; industry contributes 27%, and agriculture just 2.3% of GDP.

Australia is in the very high category of the HDI, with a value of 0.951, placing it 5th in the world.

Australia is rich in fossil fuel reserves, primarily coal but also small quantities of oil and gas. These resources translate into a fossil-dominated electricity supply, with over 50% of the total of 268 TWh in 2021 being coal generation and a further 20% gas generation. The low carbon sectors – hydroelectricity and renewables – contribute the remaining 30%, with both solar and wind making the main contributions.

Water resources and demand

Overall, Australia is very well endowed with water. Annual freshwater withdrawals are just 3% of the internal resources, and the renewable water resource per capita is just under 20,000 m³, considerably higher than the world average of 15,000; the water stress level has fallen by a factor of two over the last 30 years and now stands at a very low 5%. In terms of the CRI, Australia ranked 19th in the world in 2019, worse than the average ranking of 31st over the first two decades of this century.

The overall position, then, is healthy in terms of resources, but some of the trends tell a different story. For example, Australia's total annual rainfall in 2019–2020 was 347 mm, about 100 mm below the long-term (1900–2020) average; also, the country experienced the driest 24-month period recorded in the previous two years.

There are also marked differences between States. The lower rainfall resulted in low flow in some rivers across southern Australia, and storage in this region remained low over an extended period. Stream flows in southwest Western Australia were also below average in 2019–2020 due to very low average winter rainfall. Data for this region show the continued decline in average streamflow that has been occurring for over 100 years, from about 350 million m³ in 1900 to just 50 million m³ in 2020.

Agriculture consumes most of the water withdrawals, about 67% of the 14 billion m³ for 2019–2020; industry consumed 11% and urban centres 22% of the total. The water consumed is mostly sourced from surface water, with 75% of the 14 billion m³ consumed; groundwater, desalinated water, and inter-regional transfers make up the rest, with 20%, 4%, and 1% of the total respectively.

Desalination in Australia

The desalination sector in Australia is made up of around 270 desalination plants, most of which are small-scale. There are six large plants all built since 2006 to improve water security for coastal cities, for example, Perth in Western Australia, Adelaide in South Australia, Sydney in New South Wales, and Brisbane in Queensland. Maximum plant capacity varies from about

125,000 m³ per day to over 400,000 m³ per day, or 45 million m³ per year to 150 million m³ per year, respectively. The total capacity of the six plants is just under 1.5 million m³ per day, or about 530 million m³ per year; this is 4% of the total water consumed in Australia in 2019–2020. RO using seawater feed is the technology deployed for these modern plants.

The total capacity of all 270 desalination plants amounts to about 880 million m³ per year and uses both seawater and brackish water. The total capacity of the sector without the six largest plants, then, is 350 million m³ per year; the average capacity of the 264 or so small plants is 1.4 million m³ per year, or about 3,500 m³ per day.

Perth is perhaps the city most exposed to water scarcity. This has been brought about by population growth and the impact of changing climate; the population has grown by a factor of 7 since 1950 to over 2 million people in 2022, and during this same period, rainfall has collapsed by a factor of 7 to just 50 million m³ per year. The city has two desalination plants, which provided almost half the city's needs in 2019–2020; the city also draws on its groundwater resources.

New desalination plants are in various stages of development: Belmont and Kangaroo Island in New South Wales and Eyre Peninsular in South Australia. The new plant in Belmont will have a capacity of 30,000 m³ per day, providing drinking water for a region suffering from regular droughts. The facility on Kangaroo Island is needed to improve drinking water security for the local and tourist communities and to support agriculture; it will also provide water for fire-fighting use. The local community objected to the location of the Eyre Peninsular desalination project, and the utility is exploring alternative sites for its plant.

5.3   Overview key findings

Table 5.1 below provides some observations from the country case studies across different aspects of the desalination industry. It highlights the key drivers beyond the size of a country's population and its economic well-being, a confirmation of the 'winning' desalination technologies, the nature of the feedwater, and how the pure water produced is used. It also highlights which energy sources are preferred in a world where conventional fossil sources are expensive and new low-carbon technologies have emerged.

Each of the country case studies highlights a different feature of the industry: playing an essential role in the provision of pure water in Saudi Arabia and Israel to contingency use in the UK; from a mature and stable industry in Spain to a relatively new and fast-growing sector in China; and from the exploitation of seawater resources in Chile to the predominate use of brackish feedwater in Morocco and the USA. The economics of water production and the price of water to consumers also differ across countries, determined by local factors and the enabling framework provided by the government.

Table 5.1 Some observations across the country case studies

Country	Key driver[1]	Technology adopted	Dominant feed water	Desalinated water use	Source of energy	Additional comments
Saudi Arabia	Over exploitation groundwater resources	MSF, RO, MED	Sea	Domestic	Fossil fuels for thermal energy and electricity	Low energy and water costs to consumer
Israel	Semi-arid environment and variable rainfall	RO	Sea	Domestic	Fossil fuel for electricity	Reduced renewable freshwater withdrawals
Morocco	Poor water quality and drought conditions	RO	Brackish	Domestic Agriculture	Fossil fuel electricity Low carbon electricity	Plans for 20 operational plants by mid-2030s
Spain	Regular and extended droughts	RO	Sea Brackish	Domestic	Renewable energy in a balanced mix	Has developed a strong supply chain capability
Cyprus	Supplement variable rainfall	RO	Sea	Domestic	Fossil fuel electricity	Total plant capacity not always exploited
UK	Contingency in drought conditions	RO	River estuary. Seasonal salinity	Domestic	Gas generation. Low carbon electricity	Single plant. Local opposition to a new plant
USA	Supplements renewable sources	RO	Brackish	Domestic	All sources. State dependent	Desalination used in 35 of 50 States
Chile	Lack of freshwater in North Chile	RO	Sea	Industry Domestic	Renewable fossil fuel electricity	Major new build programme
China	Water stress increase	RO, MED	Sea	Domestic	Coal generation Low carbon electricity	Large build programme. New water infrastructure
Australia	Low rainfall and drought periods in some States	RO	Sea Brackish	Domestic	Fossil generation Low carbon electricity	New plants planned. Local opposition to one plant

Notes: (1), Drivers beyond social and economic drivers. RO, Reverse Osmosis; MSF, Multi-Stage Flash Distillation; MED, Multi-Effect Distillation.

Viewed together, the observations in this table provide some indications on the status of the industry across very different jurisdictions; they provide some insights into the next stage of the evolution of the industry and the key themes that are emerging.

Summary key points

- Water stress is affecting countries in all parts of the world, driven by social and economic factors and increasingly exacerbated by climate change.
- A lack of renewable freshwater resources and unsustainable use of groundwater resources are important drivers of desalination in many countries, particularly in the Middle East and North Africa region.
- An increasing incidence of drought conditions makes desalination a necessary, if expensive, option in many countries around the world.
- There are plans to build new desalination facilities to supplement freshwater resources in most of the country case studies selected. New desalination plants will also be needed to replace existing facilities that will be decommissioned over the next 20 years.
- The country case studies confirm that RO is now the preferred technology, in part due to its low energy consumption but also because the technology can be readily adopted and scaleable, is flexible in the way it can be used, and is easily maintained.
- Countries exploit both seawater and brackish water resources to produce pure water, mostly to provide additional drinking water in the domestic sector and, in a few cases, for irrigation in the agriculture sector and in industry; in a very few cases, replenishment of aquifers and water storage facilities also occurs.
- The combustion of fossil fuels, either directly to produce thermal energy for plants, or indirectly to produce electricity also used in plants, remains the dominant energy source. However, low-carbon electricity in the form of hydroelectricity and nuclear generation via the grid and wind and solar technologies integrated on or close to desalination sites is increasingly being used.
- The desalination industry – developers and operators, and the supply chain – has matured over the last two decades, giving confidence to decision-makers that it can meet the freshwater challenge faced by countries across the world. This has encouraged plans for major new build programmes in all regions of the world and the promise of more widespread technical capability and industrial capacity.

6 Desalination in the future

The production capacity of the desalination industry will grow significantly over the next 30 years as freshwater demand continues to grow and water scarcity increases.

6.1 Looking ahead to 2050

It is not possible to try to predict what will happen in the medium- to long-term future. However, it is possible to use scenario analysis to explore possible futures by considering how underlying economic, social, and technical developments might evolve individually and collectively. Such scenarios have been used by a variety of organisations around the world to gain greater insights into, for example, energy and environmental issues and to help inform decision-makers, from policy development to investment decisions. Such organisations have included global institutions such as the United Nations Environment Programme (UNEP), academic institutions such as the International Institute for Applied Systems Analysis (IIASA), non-government organisations (NGOs) such as Greenpeace, and commercial organisations such as Shell International.

The most common scenarios have focused on the nature and scale of energy consumption in the coming decades and the implications for greenhouse gas emissions. Meteorologists can use these emissions to model the resultant atmospheric radiative forcing and temperature variations, and the associated changes in climate around the world over and above the existing natural variability. An understanding of the possible impacts on, for example, freshwater resources and future action follows. Increasing computer power over the last 20 years or so has meant a much more granular approach can be adopted, and the models can now be applied to carry out sub-country-level analysis, making them more useful to decision-makers.

Model outputs are only useful if there is confidence in the exogenous inputs. The most *convincing* scenarios are those that weave together the complex interactions between economic, social, and technical developments. The most *compelling* scenarios are those that describe future developments in the form of strong narratives, underpinned by detailed model projections

DOI: 10.4324/9781003334224-6

consistent with these narratives. The number of scenarios is relatively unimportant; rather, it is the scope of coverage that is important, and this can be achieved with as few as two or three scenarios.

6.1.1 Scenario analyses: Context

IIASA, in their study *Water Futures and Solutions Initiative*, published in 2016, used multi-disciplinary scenario analysis to better understand the current and future water situation around the world. This work was carried out in the period from 2010–2015 and much has happened in the period to 2023; nonetheless, the analysis remains helpful since the underlying trends over the long term are broadly unchanged. This analysis drew on expert knowledge gained over many years through, for example, the assessment work of the Intergovernmental Panel on Climate Change (IPCC) and state-of-the-art climate, socio-economic, and hydrological models to examine possible water futures to the milestone date of 2050 and beyond; this helped create consistency across the various sectoral scenarios.

The IIASA process focused on three scenarios – *Sustainability, Middle of the Road,* and *Regional Rivalry* – and the implications for a range of uses for water. The general trends described in these scenarios are like those used in other scenario exercises over the years.

In *Sustainability*, the world is making progress in meeting development goals, reducing resource intensity, and fossil fuel dependency; it is characterised by an open, globalised economy with technological change directed towards environmentally friendly processes in, for example, energy supply and agriculture. The United Nations Millennium Development Goals (now evolved to the Sustainable Development Goals since 2015) are met in the coming decades with educated populations having access to safe water, sanitation, and medical care.

In the *Middle of the Road* scenario, the world continues much as before, following trends typical of recent years and decades, with some progress towards achieving development goals; resource and energy intensity is lower than historic level and there is a decreasing dependency on fossil fuels. Achievement of the Millennium Development Goals is delayed by several decades, leaving populations without access to safe water, sanitation, and medical care.

Regional Rivalry is a world of regions with little international cooperation and coordination; there remains extreme poverty and pockets of moderate wealth, and many countries struggle to maintain living standards for their growing populations. This is a world failing to achieve global development goals, with countries focusing on achieving energy and food security within their own region. The world has de-globalised, and international trade, including energy resources and agricultural markets, is severely restricted.

The energy and water sectors are intimately linked. Water is used across the energy spectrum, from fossil fuel extraction to electricity production, and energy is essential for water abstraction from the surface and groundwater resources and for its treatment and delivery to end-users. Developments in one sector have an impact on the other. The International Energy Agency (IEA) publishes a World Energy Outlook (WEO) each year, focusing on the energy supply and the allied industries of power, transport, and water. The IIASA analysis drew on the WEO 2015 study for their analysis, and it is these that are presented here for consistency; they address the period to 2040 rather than 2050.

Once again, three possible future pathways are described: *Current Policies Scenario, New Policy Scenarios*, and *450 Scenario*. As with all scenarios, the names given help describe the world in the future. The first scenario adopts those policies that affect energy markets up to 2015, while the second scenario includes declared policies that are due to be implemented in the years following this milestone date. The third scenario describes the policies and measures whereby carbon dioxide (CO_2) emissions result in 450 parts per million (ppm) in the atmosphere in 2050, a value that climate models predict would limit temperature rises to less than 2°C.

6.1.2 Scenario analysis: Economic and social drivers

The IIASA scenario analysis provides many valuable insights into the way in which the world may evolve in the period to 2050 and beyond, focusing on drivers in the water industry and their implications for water resources. For example, economic and social developments are important drivers for the way in which water resources are used; they include population growth, the nature and scale of economies, productivity gains in agriculture and food production, and electricity supply which has emerged as the dominant energy carrier this century.

Population and Gross Domestic Product

The analysis projects the world's population will rise to between 8.4 and 9.8 billion in the 2050s, depending on scenario. The lower value of 8.4 million is that for *Sustainability*, which is also the population peak before declining in this scenario; the higher value of 9.8 billion is that for *Regional Rivalry* and in this scenario, the population continues to rise to 2100 and beyond. The population in Asia is by far the largest, at around 5 billion, followed by that in Africa at about 2 billion for the *Middle of the Road* scenario; however, Asia's population has peaked by the middle of the century, while that for Africa continues to rise in this scenario. Europe's population is stable at about 750 million in the period to 2050 and then slowly declines to the end of the century.

The world's GDP also continues to grow throughout this century. By 2050, GDP in *Sustainability* rises to just under $300 trillion, using Purchasing Power Parity (PPP) and in constant $2005, which is three times that for 2020; the GDP for *Middle of the Road* is about $220 trillion in 2050, just over a factor of two greater than in 2020, while that for *Regional Rivalry* is lower at around

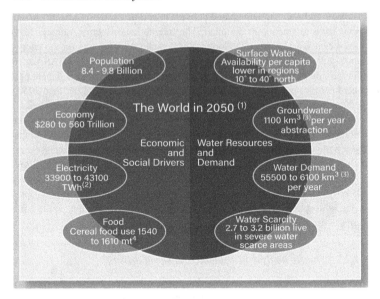

Figure 6.1 The world in 2050

Source: (1), Water Futures and Solutions, Peter Burek, IIASA, 2016.

Notes: (2), Model predictions for electricity sector in 2040; (3), one billion m³; (4) mt, million tonnes.

$180 trillion. In all cases Asia makes the largest contribution to GDP in 2050, greater than the combined value in Europe, North and South America.

Food production

Agriculture and food production rely heavily on water resources. A growing world population and increased wealth in many regions need more food production and a greater emphasis on better nutrition and protein-rich diets. Average global food energy intake in 2010 was about 2,860 kcal per capita per day, rising to between 2,950 and 3,360 kcal per capita per day for *Regional Rivalry Scenario* and the *Sustainability Scenario* respectively.

Cereals play an important role in human diets, providing starch and protein, dietary fibre, and nutrients; they are also used in animal feed. Global cereal food and feed were estimated to be 1,145 and 930 million tonnes, respectively in 2010. Cereal food use is projected to rise to between 1,540 and 1,610 million tonnes in 2050, depending on the scenario, while cereal feed use rises to between 1,380 and 1,500 million tonnes, again depending on the scenario.

The increased need for global food and feed in the coming decades will place further demands on land, water, and energy resources and further degrade the natural environment. The area of cultivated land – defined as arable land and land under permanent crops – will rise from a total of 1,540 million hectares in 2010 to between 1,620 and 1,775 million hectares in 2050. To put these figures into context, this is about the same as the total land area of the Russian Federation. Land under irrigation was estimated at just over 320 million hectares in 2010 and rises to between 355 and 375 million hectares in 2050. Again, to put this into context, this is similar to the combined land area of Argentina and Chile. The water used for irrigation was estimated at 2,340 km^3 per year in 2010, rising to between 2,870 and 3,310 km^3 per year in 2050; this amounts to an increase of 23% to 42% above the level used in 2010.

Energy and water

The 2015 WEO study suggests that primary energy demand grows by 13%–45% between 2010 and 2040, depending on scenario, with the smallest rise in the *450 Scenario,* as expected since this is constrained by the need to meet the 450 ppm CO_2 target in the atmosphere. However, fossil fuels - coal, oil, and gas – continue to make major contributions, independent of scenario. Primary energy demand growth is most evident in countries and regions with large and growing populations, such as India, China, Africa, Southeast Asia, and the Middle East. The power sector continues to be the major energy end-use sector, accounting for over 60% of coal demand and 40% of gas demand; it also accounts for over 40% of global energy-related CO_2 emissions.

Electricity demand grows faster than primary energy, reflecting the importance of this form of energy for rising populations and increased access; economic activity, the electrification of major sectors such as transport and domestic heat, and growth in the digital economy are also important drivers. Major increases in electricity demand take place in India, Southeast Asia, and Africa with an annual growth rate in these regions of 4% per annum.

Global electricity generation, then, is projected to increase significantly from just under 23,500 TWh in 2010 to between 34,000 TWh and 43,000 TWh in 2040, again depending on the scenario. A major shift in technology deployed is also observed in this period. The contribution from fossil fuels to total electricity generation decreases from 77% of the total (or 15,740 Wh) in 2010 to a best-case scenario of 29% (or 9,850 TWh) in 2040. Generation from the low-carbon sector grows significantly. The renewable technologies are projected to deliver just under 18,000 TWh by 2040 in the best-case scenario, with hydroelectricity being the largest contributor. Generation from wind and solar technologies grow at the fastest rate, facilitated by government subsidies and a decline in production costs; nuclear generation also increases by up to 150% (or 6,200 TWh) by 2040. The decarbonisation of the electricity sector also has beneficial implications for the water industry, with its energy-related emissions also falling.

The growing demand for energy in general, and particularly electricity, also has major implications for water resources. Water withdrawals for global energy production were estimated at over 580 km^3 (or 580 billion m^3) in 2010, which amounted to about 15% of the total withdrawals; 90% of these were used in electricity production. The trend is for increased water use by the energy sector in the period to 2035 across all scenarios, from a low of 600 km^3 in the *450 ppm* scenario to a high of 790 km^3 in the *Current Policies* scenario. The move away from electricity production by coal-fired technology and the increased electricity production from renewables are strong drivers for lower water consumption in the sector in the longer term.

The mainstream electricity sector is dependent on both the ready availability and a stable temperature of the water it uses; climate change will affect both in many parts of the world. The USA, southern and central Europe, Southeast Asia, southern parts of South America, northern and southern parts of Africa, and southern Australia will have lower natural freshwater flows in the coming decades, and these will reduce the output of both hydroelectric plants and thermal power systems. The effects can be mitigated to some extent by increasing the performance of the plants, the adoption of renewable technologies, and, in some jurisdictions, the continued use of nuclear power.

6.1.3   Scenario analysis: Water resources and demand

As indicated earlier, the IIASA scenario analysis provides many valuable insights into the way in which the world may evolve in the period to 2050. In the sections above, the focus was on economic and social developments in the coming decades, while the following sections focused on the implications for surface and groundwater resources and water demand and scarcity.

Surface and groundwater resources

The scenario analysis above suggests the period to 2050 sees significant rises in population, GDP, electricity demand, and food production. Surface water availability, at least at the global and regional level, remains relatively stable, with the former estimated at over 50,000 km^3 per year. To put this volume into context, the largest freshwater lakes by volume are Baikal in Southern Siberia (23,600 km^3), Tanganyika in Africa (18,900 km^3) and Superior in North America (12,000 km^3); the total amount of water held in these lakes is 54,500 km^3. Differences at the regional level amount to no more than +/- 5% in the period to 2050 and beyond, but there are larger differences seen at the country level.

The available water resources per capita is one indicator used to describe water scarcity. A value of >1,700 m^3 per capita per year suggests there is no water stress in a country, while a value of between 500 and 1,000 suggests scarcity conditions; a value of <500 can be described as absolute scarcity. The scenario analysis suggests that water availability per capita will decrease in regions that lie between 0° and 40° northern latitude, including countries from Morocco to India and beyond. At the macro level, some countries, like the USA, may not be classified as water stressed, but they have some regions where water availability is a major challenge.

Groundwater is a very important source of water around the world, particularly in arid regions where, for example, drinking water is needed for growing populations or where agriculture remains a key sector; this source also provides a valuable reserve in periods of drought. Groundwater abstraction amounted to an estimated 800 km³ per year in the second decade of this century, almost 70% of which was in just five countries: India, the USA, China, Iran, and Pakistan. In many countries, such abstraction is not sustainable with overexploitation of aquifers. Nonetheless, there is an expectation that by 2050, groundwater abstractions will increase to 1,100 km³ per year with the same five countries dominating; this is equivalent to draining the freshwater equivalent of lake Michigan in North America every year.

Water demand

The IIASA analysis suggests global water demand continues to grow in all scenarios. The total estimated demand will be between 5,500 and 6,100 km³ per year in 2050, some 20–30% higher than the demand of 4,600 km³ per year in 2010; to put these figures into context, the total freshwater volume contained in the three North American lakes of Huron, Ontario, and Erie combined is 5,660 km³.

At the regional level, the contribution by Asia to global water demand today is very high at about 65% and is projected to remain at about this level in the period to 2050; beyond Asia, North and Central America, and Europe have the next largest demand with 14% and 10%, respectively, and their contributions will fall slightly in the same period to the middle of the century. Africa and South America will see a large increase in demand brought about by growing populations, increased economic development, and rising incomes; the smallest increases in demand will be in Oceania, North, and Central America.

At the country level, the largest water demand occurs in China, India, the USA, Russia, and Pakistan, and this will continue to be the case in the period to 2050. Many countries in Africa will see major increases in demand, perhaps by a factor of six, in the same period.

Water demand at the global level is dominated by the agriculture sector, which accounts for just over 70% of the total; industry and domestic water demand account for just under 20% and 10%, respectively. Looking ahead to 2050, the total demand is 3,477, 1,381, and 967 km³ per year for the agriculture, industry, and domestic sectors, respectively; these projections suggest the distribution changes slightly, with the demand by the agriculture sector falling in this period to 60% and that for the industry and the domestic sectors rising to 24% and 17%, respectively.

Water demand for agriculture, then, continues to dominate in many regions around the world, the exception being Europe, where agriculture accounts for just 30% of the total. However, at the global level, its contribution falls in the period to 2050, the exception being the North and Central America region, where the percentage contribution to the total remains about the same. Industrial water demand increases across all regions, particularly in Asia and Africa, except for North and Central America, which experience a marked decline. In absolute terms, demand for water in the domestic sector increases in all regions, from a factor of 1.3 in Europe to a factor of 3.9 in Africa.

Water scarcity

Water scarcity is being driven by rising populations, increasing demand for food production, economic development, and changing patterns of water supply. One indicator is the available water resources per capita; another is the annual withdrawals compared to supply. Regions are considered water scarce if annual withdrawals are between 20% and 40% of the annual supply, and severely water scarce if withdrawals are greater than 40%. Some regions, such as Western South America and North Africa, and countries like Mexico, northeast Brazil, Chile, Afghanistan, Pakistan, India, northeast China, southwest Australia, and South Africa, are already suffering under water scarce conditions. In the period to 2050, more regions are projected to experience severe water scarcity conditions: northern and southern Africa, the Middle East, central, and eastern Asia.

These conditions mean that on an annual basis, an estimated 1.9 billion people, or 27% of the total world population, currently live in regions that suffer from severe water scarcity conditions; this number is projected to increase to between 2.7 and 3.2 billion people, depending on the scenario. However, an estimated 3.6 billion people are currently living in this scarcity category based on the most water scarce month, and this rises to between 4.8 and 5.7 billion by 2050; this means that almost 60% of the world's population will live in regions of severe water scarcity for at least one month each year. The water industry, then, faces some major challenges, and the desalination industry offers a technological solution, along with other measures that will be needed, to deliver pure water on the scale required.

Cost of desalinated water

Cost remains a major barrier to desalination technology being deployed, particularly in the less developed countries. The International Water Association (IWA) presented an analysis of the possible cost evolution of desalinated water by Reverse Osmosis (RO) in 2016, as shown in Table 6.1. They believed that average plant construction costs would decline by 60% in the period to the mid-2030s, while the cost of electricity use in production would decline by 40%; also, innovations in membrane technology would improve their productivity by almost 300%. Such cost progress translates to an average cost of desalinated water that is 60% lower than that in 2016, making the technology more widely available.

Table 6.1 Projected cost of desalinated water

Parameter		Units	2016	Within 5 years	Within 20 years
Key economic drivers	Construction cost	US$ per MLD	1.2–2.2	1.0–1.8	0.5–0.9
	Electrical energy	kWh per m³	3.5–4.0	2.8–3.2	2.1–2.4
	Membrane productivity	m³ per membrane	28–47	35–55	95–120
	Cost of water	US$ per m³	0.8–1.2	0.6–1.0	0.3–0.5

Source: Desalination – Past Present and Future, IWA, August 2016.

Note: MLD, million litres per day or 1,000 m³ per day.

It is important that technical institutions and the supply chain are encouraged to bring forward innovations to make the projected decline in the cost of desalinated water a reality. This would allow many less developed countries suffering from water stress to deploy the technology.

6.2 Potential evolution of the desalination industry to 2050

The scenario analyses discussed above provide an indication of how the key drivers for water resources might evolve and interact over the next three decades at the regional and country levels. They also provide a changing context for the desalination industry going forward.

6.2.1 *Converging developments for the desalination industry*

There are converging developments that will determine the future of this technology: the scale and distribution of population growth, the resources available, the emergence of a dominant technology, innovation and declining costs, increased energy diversity, the provision of financial incentives, new entrants into the market, and protection of the environment.

Such developments, expressed in Table 6.2, are helpful in determining whether desalination remains a small contributor at the global level but continues to play an important role in some countries or grows to be an essential part of the water supply infrastructure, servicing many hundreds of millions of people in a world of climate change.

Several studies have discussed the development of the desalination industry over the last 50 years or so. A distinction is made between those desalination plants that have been constructed and those that are operational. It is also worth noting that the volume of water produced by each operational plant in

Table 6.2 Converging developments for greater deployment of desalination technology

Theme	Trend	Outcome
Societal	Population continues to grow to the middle of the century	Greater demand for energy food and water, including desalinated water
	Transition from rural to urban centres continues in developing countries	Desalination easier to integrate into water supply infrastructure
Resources	Traditional sources of water under pressure	Alternative sources of water needed to meet demand
	Water storage and transport infrastructure improvements	Eases integration of desalination into the water infrastructure
Technology	Key desalination technologies emerging	Reverse Osmosis is the technology of choice
	Global supply chain emerging with new entrants	Increasing deployment and operations capability
Economics	Desalination costs and price of pure water decline	Innovation, efficiency, and scale drive cost reduction
	Sector seen to have major investment possibilities	Potential for new entrants into the market
Energy	Innovations by the supply chain deliver energy efficiency gains	Decline in energy per unit of pure water produced
	Energy diversity increases and pure water production a storage medium	Renewable technologies replace fossil fuels as main energy providers
Environment	Average global temperature increases, leading to climate change	Water scarcity more widespread and increasing severity in some regions
	Global and local environment concerns	Abatement technology adopted and brine waste converted to useful products

Source: Author's assessment.

any one year may not be the same as its nameplate capacity; this is because the scale of plant output contracted with the relevant government agency may not be at its maximum due to the availability, or otherwise, of alternative sources of water provision.

6.2.2 *Status of desalination industry*

Desalination plant size has gradually increased over the years, driven by new technology and the desperate need for water in some water-scarce countries. A recent analysis finds there were almost 20,000 plants in 2020, with about 16,000 operational. The overall production capacity available is much closer because the average size of plants has increased over time; the total nameplate capacity of the plants constructed was over 100 million m^3 per day, while the operational capacity is almost 95 million m³ per day. The latter is almost 35 billion m³ or 35 km³ each year, which is about the same volume of water that flows over the Victoria Falls in Zimbabwe each year.

The growth rate in desalination capacity has declined over the decades, a common occurrence in many industries as it has evolved and matured. In the early development phase of the industry, the growth rate was over 20% per annum in the period 1980–1990, albeit from a very low base. The growth rate over the next two decades was over 10% per annum; by 2010, there were almost 15,000 plants built with 11,000 in operation. The growth rate declined further over the next ten years, from just under 9% in the period 2010–2015 to 4.5% in the period 2015–2020.

What has become evident over the last couple of decades is that the 'winning' technology has emerged in the form of Reverse Osmosis (RO) which now makes up almost 70% of operational plants. RO plants are relatively easy to deploy, use electricity, and can be scaled to match local needs. Looking ahead, it is possible that this technology, or more efficient versions, will continue to dominate the sector while those that rely on the more energy-intensive thermal processes will likely decline, albeit gradually, in the Middle East, where fossil fuel energy remains plentiful and cheap.

6.2.3 Analytical approach adopted for the period 2020–2050

The following sections summarise the approach adopted for the author's scenario analysis. It provides the basis for the pure water production capacity projections to 2050 and an estimate of the number of additional new desalination plants that may be built to deliver the capacity in that period. The analysis also considers the existing fleet and discusses the potential gradual replacement of plants as they retire. The electricity needed to deliver the projected plant capacity can also be calculated along with the associated carbon dioxide emissions and brine waste production.

Below is the rationale underpinning the analysis for each of the metrics involved:

1) Desalination capacity production

As indicated above, historical data is available for the desalination industry for the period 1980–2020. A simple analysis suggests the following growth rates: 20.5% average annual growth in the decade 1980–1990, 10.2% during 1990–2000, 10.45% during 2000–2010, 8.75% for 2010–2015, and 4.5% growth for the period 2015–2020. Two scenarios are suggested by the author to gain further insights into the possible development of the industry in the future: one, called the *Heroic* scenario, continues the 4.5% per annum growth for the period 2020–2050 and a second, called the *Progressive* scenario, continues the longer-term decline in growth with 2% per annum for that period. Of course, 30 years is a long period of time, and it is possible that the industry begins the period at 4.5% and gradually declines to 2% by 2050.

2) Number of new plants

The analysis focuses on plants added in the period 2020–2050 and assumes that all new plants use RO technology; it also assumes the average capacity of RO plant grows from just under 7,000 m^3 per day in 2020 to almost 20,000 m^3 per day in 2050. Further, new plants are needed to replace those that are closed at the end of their lifetime, and these are similarly assumed to be RO technology and follow the same growth in average capacity.

3) Electricity and thermal energy consumption

All the mainstream technologies have been deployed in the period 1980–2020 but RO is increasingly the technology of choice, particularly in countries where indigenous fossil fuel supplies are not available and renewable technologies can be deployed. Values for water production by technology for 2020 confirm that RO technology amounts to almost 70% of the total.

There are a range of values for the electricity consumption of the various desalination technologies; the electricity consumed by the sector in this author analysis assumes an average value of 4 kWh per m^3 and for simplicity, this remains unchanged throughout the 2020–2050 period. It is worth noting that this value will likely go down as further innovations and efficiency gains in operations are realised.

Thermal energy is needed for several technologies, and, once again, a range of values have been reported. The electrical equivalent for each technology is used in the analysis; for example, an average value of 25 kWh per m^3 is used for Multi-Stage Flash (MSF) technology. In both scenarios, the thermal energy is assumed to decline to zero in the period to 2050 as operational plants that use this technology are closed, and all new plants are assumed to use RO technology.

4) Carbon dioxide emissions

Having established the freshwater projections from desalination and the associated electricity and thermal energy, it is possible to calculate the carbon dioxide emissions associated with the pure water produced. The estimated CO_2 emissions associated with water produced by each technology have been reported in $kgCO_2$ per m^3; it is possible, then, to establish a baseline value of CO_2 emissions for the sector in 2020 using the water production capacity by technology. The component associated with the thermal technologies, such as Multi-Stage Flash (MSF), are then assumed to decline to zero in the period to 2050; CO_2 emissions beyond 2020 are assumed to be from technologies like RO that rely solely on electricity.

The CO_2 emissions of the electricity sector, by region, is available for the period to 2050 in $kgCO_2$ per kWh (the carbon intensity). Using the desalination capacity in each region, it is possible to calculate a weighted average $kgCO_2$ per kWh for use at the global level. The electricity-related CO_2

emissions from the sector are derived by the product of the projected electricity consumption in each of the two scenarios and the carbon intensity.
5) Brine waste production
  There is good historical data on the estimated volume of brine produced for every cubic metre of pure water by technology. The brine production going forward is calculated from the product of the projected pure water produced in each scenario and the volume of brine produced per cubic metre factor.

To summarise, this scenario analysis relies on a simple analytical approach, starting with the projected total water production capacity over time; it also uses the production by technology in the most recent years. The electricity consumed by each technology is used to estimate the total electricity required by the sector, as is the electrical equivalent of the thermal energy used for selected technologies. The resulting total carbon dioxide emissions (CO_2) from operating plants is calculated using the carbon intensity ($kgCO_2$ per kWh), and the quantity of brine waste produced is similarly calculated based on its production per m^3 of pure water produced.

6.2.4   *Potential desalination production capacity*

Two possible futures, then, are suggested by the author based on different growth rates in the period 2020–2050: the *Heroic* scenario assumes continuation of the recent growth rate of about 4.5% per annum while the *Progressive* scenario describes a future where the growth rate of 2% per annum is used, consistent with the observed gradual decline in rate for the desalination industry and other technologies over the medium to long term.

As indicated in Chapter 4, pure water produced by desalination is primarily used to service the needs of the domestic sector. The IIASA analysis provides projections of regional water demand for this sector in 2050, consistent with social, economic, and environmental developments described in their scenarios; Table 6.3 draws on these projections to put the author's scenario outcomes into context.

In the *Heroic* scenario, the desalination capacity increases from around 95 million m^3 per day in 2020 to around 355 million m^3 per day in 2050, an increase by just under a factor of 4; the total annual production capacity from the sector would amount to 130 billion m^3 or 130 km^3 of pure water, which is the volume of freshwater contained in Lake Albert in Africa; this volume amounts to about 13.5% of the projected global domestic demand in 2050.

The total projected capacity in the *Progressive* scenario is 188 million m^3 per year in 2050, or about twice that in 2020, and the annual production is almost 70 km^3 of pure water; this is about the same annual volume of water that flows over Niagara Falls and amounts to about 7% of the projected domestic demand, unchanged from the percentage contribution in 2020. Viewed another way, the production capacity of the sector in this scenario would need to grow at 2%

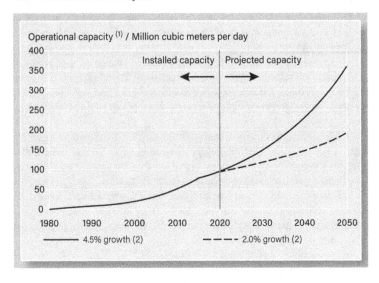

Figure 6.2 Potential operational desalination capacity to 2050

Source: Installed operational capacity from The state of desalination and brine production, Edward Jones et al., Science of the Total Environment, Volume 657, pp1343–1356, 2019.

Note: (1), Observed annual growth rates of operational capacity are: 20% for the period 1980 to 1990; 10% for the period 1990 to 2010; 9% for the period 2010 to 2015; 4.5 % is the continuation of recent growth while 2% is a more conservative growth (author's analysis, see text).

each year for the desalination sector to continue with the same percentage contribution to global domestic supply in 2050 as in 2020.

There are countries in each region already suffering from water scarcity to a lesser or greater extent. Going forward, the water demand projections in Table 6.3 suggest that some countries in northern and southern Africa, the

Table 6.3 Water demand for the domestic sector in the IIASA *Middle of the Road* scenario

Region	2010 km³	2050 km³	2010 % of total	2050 % of total	2050:2010 % increase
Africa	26	101	6.1	10.4	388
Asia	202	565	47.3	58.4	280
North and Central America	82	118	19.2	12.2	144
South America	39	82	9.1	8.5	210
Europe	72	93	16.9	9.6	129
Oceania	6	9	1.4	0.9	150
World	427	967	n/a	n/a	226

Source: Adapted from *Water Futures and Solution Initiative*, Peter Burak et al., IIASA, 2016.

Middle East, and central and eastern Asia will experience severe water scarcity. It is reasonable, then, to assume that the greatest need for desalination will occur in Asia, including the Middle East, which accounts for almost 60% of global domestic water demand and, in absolute terms, will have trebled its needs in the period 2010–2050. Other regions, including North and South Africa, and parts of North and Central America, will also see their need for desalination production grow significantly in this period.

6.2.5 Potential number of desalination plants

The implications of the projected growth and production capacity for the size of the global fleet of plants is an important consideration. The average plant size differs by technology but has grown steadily over the last 25 years for all technologies; learning curve analysis suggests that MSF and Multi-Effect Distillation (MED) are closer to their optimum plant size, while that for RO has potential to grow significantly over the next 30 years. The average capacity of plant additions for MSF and MED in 2020 is 88,000 and 20,000 m³ per day, respectively. The average capacity of plant additions for RO plants is lower at just under 7,000 m³ per day but is projected to rise to just under 20,000 m³ per day by 2050 (see Table 6.4).

The heroic and progressive scenarios

As indicated in Chapter 3, there is a very strong case to suggest that RO technology is the 'winning' technology for desalination, as evidenced by its rapid

Table 6.4 Mainstream desalination technology attributes in the period 2015 to 2050[1]

Attribute	Technology	Historical 2015	Projected 2020	Projected 2050
Cumulative installed capacity (Million m³ per day)	Reverse Osmosis	56.1	79.2	143.5
	Multi-Stage Flash	17.5	18.7	20.7
	Multi-Effect Distillation	6.4	7.6	10.3
	Total	80.1	105.5	174.6
Cumulative installed units	Reverse Osmosis	24842	29263	36842
	Multi-Stage Flash	1579	1579	1592
	Multi-Effect Distillation	2158	2237	2368
	Total	28579	33079	40803
Average capacity of unit additions (Thousand m³ per day)	Reverse Osmosis	5.3	7.0	19.5
	Multi-Stage Flash	81.4	90.7	100.0
	Multi-Effect Distillation	15.5	20.7	25.1

Source: (1), Multidimensional analysis of nexus technologies I: diffusion, scaling and cost trends of desalination, B. Mayor, June 2018, IIASA.

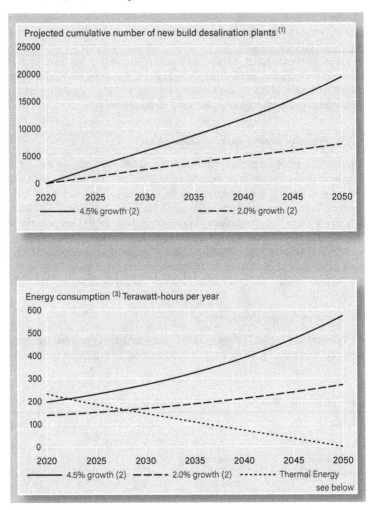

Figure 6.3 Potential number of new plants and energy consumption to 2050

Notes (Upper chart): (1), Uses potential plant sizes to 2050 in Multidimensional analysis of nexus technologies: diffusion, scaling and cost trends in desalination, B Mayor, IIASA, 2018; does not include new plants to replace existing plants in 2020 which will likely close in the period to 2050; (2), author's analysis, see text. (Lower chart): (1), Uses potential plant sizes to 2050 in Multidimensional analysis of nexus technologies: diffusion, scaling and cost trends in desalination, B Mayor, IIASA, 2018; (2), author's analysis, see text; (3), uses historical operational capacity data from The state of desalination and brine production, Edward Jones et al., Science of the Total Environment, Volume 657, 2019 and energy consumption data from Integration of Wind Energy and Desalination Systems, Francesca Greco et al., ResearchGate, 2021.

growth over the last 20 years to about 70% of the current operational capacity. It is, then, possible to provide an *indicative* number of additional plants in operation over the period 2020–2050.

Assuming all future additions to the global fleet deploy RO technology, it is possible to use the projected desalination capacity in the two scenarios and the average plant capacity growth over time, to calculate the number of *additional* plants likely to be built in the period 2020–2050. This simple approach suggests the total number of additional plants in the *Heroic* scenario amounts to just over 19,000, while the number in the *Progressive* scenario is much lower at just over 7,000.

Further, the fleet production capacity in 2020 is about 95 million m^3 per day. The operational plants delivering this capacity will gradually close in the period to 2050, to be replaced by new RO plants whose average capacity will likely grow during this period, as for the additional plant estimate above. An *indicative* value for the number of *replacement* plants for the 2020 production capacity, then, is about 8,000 by 2050.

The projected total number of *additional* plants and *replacement* plants are indicative values, as new plants deployed will be of a size consistent with the needs of the communities they will serve and the attributes of the region in which they are located.

Comparison with S-curve analysis

It is important to compare these findings with other alternative approaches. Chapter 3 introduced the idea of s-curve analysis, whereby a key performance attribute of a technology is mapped against time. If this approach is applied to the global cumulative production capacity, it is possible to develop a mathematical expression that describes the s-curve evolution for each of the three main technologies: RO, MSF, and MED. IIASA carried out such an analysis in 2018 on the historical production capacity data available for the period 1990–2015 and Table 6.4 provides a summary of the results drawn from their analysis.

The projected cumulative production capacity to 2020 at about 105 million m^3 per day is very similar to other studies, and consistent with the operational value of about 95 million m^3 per day used as a starting point for the *Heroic* and *Progressive* scenarios. The cumulative projected production capacity of about 175 million m^3 per day in 2050 is close to that in the *Progressive* scenario.

The IIASA analysis also suggests a value for the cumulative number of plants of just over 40,000 by 2050; the number of additional plants over those projected for 2020 is just 7,700 with 98% using RO technology. The scale of additional plant is, once again, consistent with the *Progressive* scenario, as is the assumption that nearly all new plants post-2020 are likely to use RO technology.

Regional distribution

It is reasonable to assume that the regional distribution of new plants in the period to 2050 will, in the main, likely follow water demand for the domestic sector. The largest number of new plants, then, will be in countries in Asia, including the Middle East, and in North and South Africa; the cost of desalinated water may well be a limiting factor for deployment in the poorer countries of Africa.

6.2.6 Electricity consumption

The total electricity needed to service the sector in the *Heroic* and *Progressive* scenarios can be calculated once the projected capacity is established. The analysis requires a value for the electrical and thermal energy needed to produce a cubic metre of desalinated water. The numbers vary for both electrical and thermal energy, but since RO is increasingly being deployed in preference to the other technologies, it is reasonable to assume a value within its range of operation when considering the period 2020–2050. Assuming 95 million m^3 of desalinated water per day in 2020, and 4 kWh of electricity is needed to produce one cubic metre of water, results in a total of almost 140 TWh was needed in 2020. To put this into context, this number is comparable to the total electricity of about 152 TWh consumed in Argentina, a country of almost 46 million, in 2021.

In addition to electricity, several mainstream technologies use thermal energy in large quantities in their desalination process; these include, for example, MSF and MED technologies, which will contribute 18% and 7% of the 95 million m^3 of desalinated water per day in 2020, respectively. It is important, then, that the energy for these is also included in an assessment of the energy needs of the sector. It is possible to convert thermal energy (kJ/m^3) to electrical energy (kWh), providing an electrical equivalent of 25 kWh per m^3 of water for 'thermal' technologies such as MSF and MED; using this value means about 230 TWh equivalent was needed to deliver just 25% of the total desalinated water supplies in 2020.

Assuming that RO is the only technology deployed in the period 2020–2050 and that the thermal technologies currently in operation gradually exit, it is possible to calculate the electricity consumption by the industry in that period; in this case, the 230 TWh electrical equivalent needed for the thermal technologies in 2020, declines to zero in 2050. The electricity consumed by an RO-dominated sector in the *Heroic* scenario rises from about 140 TWh in 2020 to 520 TWh in 2050; the latter is comparable to the total electricity currently generated in France; in the *Progressive* scenario, electricity consumption grows to 275 TWh in 2050, comparable to that used in Spain.

It is also helpful to compare these values with those from previous studies. Table 6.5 summarises the results of an analysis carried out by the IEA in 2016

Table 6.5 Global electricity consumption (TWh) by process within the water industry

	Supply	Distribution	Desalination	Re-use	Wastewater treatment	Transfer	Total
2015	333	180	41	4	195	71	825
2020	352	195	56	6	222	147	979
2025	360	201	102	8	244	147	1063
2030	364	205	186	11	266	220	1252
2035	364	204	272	16	287	220	1363
2040	368	205	345	21	314	220	1473

Source: Adapted from *Water-Energy Nexus,* International Energy Agency, 2016.

Note: Supply includes ground and surface water treatment.

showing the estimated consumption by each part of the water industry, including desalination, for the period 2015–2040.

The analysis shows a significant increase in projected electricity consumption by the water industry over the next few decades. Looking ahead from 2016, when the report was published, the analysis may have underestimated the rapid growth in the desalination production capacity and the associated electricity consumption in 2020; it is much lower than then 140 TWh estimated by the authors analysis. Nonetheless, the IEA study suggests the industry grows rapidly and consumes almost a quarter of the total electricity used by the water industry, or 345 TWh, in 2040. This value is consistent with that projected for the *Heroic* scenario (335 TWh) in 2040 but very much higher than that for the *Progressive* scenario (216 TWh). The overall message, nonetheless, is that the desalination sector will grow significantly in the next few decades and its electricity consumption with it.

6.2.7 Carbon dioxide emissions

The desalination industry uses both electricity and thermal energy in its plants, and these give rise to CO_2 emissions. The calculated carbon intensity of electricity generation ($kgCO_2$ per kWh) is available at country, regional, and global levels. Additionally, the projected regional distribution of electricity generation and the associated carbon intensity are both available for the period 2020–2050; this allows a weighted average of the global carbon intensity to be calculated for this period: 0.48 million tonnes CO_2 per TWh in 2020, falling to 0.19 million tonnes CO_2 per TWh in 2050.

Using the annual projected electricity consumed by the desalination industry and the carbon intensity values provides an estimate of the carbon dioxide emissions associated with this activity. For the *Heroic* scenario then, an estimated 66 million tonnes of CO_2 were emitted in 2020, increasing to about

100 million tonnes in 2050; for the *Progressive* scenario the electricity-associated emissions fall slightly to just over 50 million tonnes in 2050.

The CO_2 emissions associated with the thermal energy used, mostly in the MSF and MED processes, must also be considered. A range of values are applicable depending on the efficiency of the process and whether it is a standalone plant or with co-generation facilities, the latter having much lower emissions. Taking the average values of standalone and co-generation plants provides a value of about 19 kg CO_2 per m^3 produced for MSF and about 12 kg CO_2 per m^3 for MED. When these emission factors are applied to the MSF and MED water production, an estimated 148 million tonnes of CO_2 were emitted in 2020.

The total estimated CO_2 emissions from the desalination industry in 2020, then, amounted to about 214 million tonnes; these are very similar to the emissions from energy use by Egypt today, a country with a population of almost 110 million. Assuming emissions from the thermal processes decline steadily to zero over the period 2020–2050, as suggested above for the desalinated water production capacity, total emissions decline to those associated with RO production in 2050: 100 and 50 million tonnes CO_2 in the *Heroic* and *Progressive* scenarios, respectively. The overall observation, then, is that CO_2 emissions from the sector may be expected to decline in the period to 2050.

6.2.8   *Brine production*

The brine waste production associated with the desalination industry was also discussed in Chapter 4. To summarise, brine production is determined by both the technology used and the feedwater available. For example, the least volume of brine waste is produced by a combination of RO and river water (RW), the most volume by MSF and SW; this is not surprising because RW has low Total Dissolved Solids (TDS), and RO removes less solids than MSF. There is, then, a good understanding of the brine waste production per cubic metre of pure water produced. As indicated earlier, the desalination industry produced about 95 million m^3 per day of pure water in 2020, and the associated brine waste produced amounted to just under 142 million m^3 per day, or almost 52 billion m^3 per year.

Looking ahead, the additional brine production in the *Heroic* and *Progressive* scenarios will be determined by the RO technology and the different feedwater options: SW, brackish water (BW), RW, and wastewater (WW). The combination RO-SW produces the most brine waste, 1.35 m^3 per m^3 of pure water produced, and the combination RO-WW produces the least, at 0.21. Considering the pure water contribution of each combination to the total, it is possible to calculate a weighted average of 1.15 m^3 brine waste per m^3 pure water in 2020.

It is, then, possible to estimate a value for the additional brine waste produced each year for the *Heroic* and *Progressive* scenarios in the period

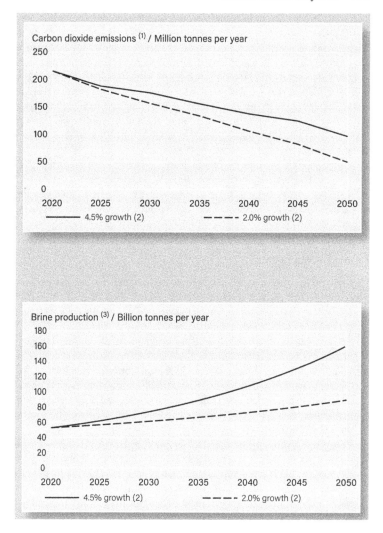

Figure 6.4 Potential carbon dioxide and brine emissions to 2050

Notes (Upper chart): (1), Uses carbon dioxide emission intensity (gCO$_2$ per kWh) in Regional CO$_2$ intensity of electricity generation worldwide from 2000 to 2050 by region, Statista, 2022; (2), 4.5 % is the continuation of recent growth while 2% is a more conservative growth, and emissions associated with the thermal energy in MED and MSF technologies are assumed to decline to zero as these technologies retire during the period (author's analysis, see text). (Lower chart): (1), Uses brine production figures in The state of desalination and brine production, E. Jones et al., Science of Total Environment, Volume 657, p1343, 2019; (2), author's analysis, see text; (3), Projected brine production made up of two components: estimated production in 2020 from all technologies plus post-2020 production assuming only Reserve Osmosis or similar technology deployed (MSF and MED plants may retire over time so the projections are likely maximum values).

2020–2050 using the total projected pure water produced by the industry and the weighted average waste production for RO above; to this must be added waste produced from the existing desalination plants in 2020, which are gradually decommissioned over the period to 2050. This simple approach suggests indicative values for the annual brine waste production of about 110 and 40 billion m³ for the *Heroic* and *Progressive* scenarios respectively in 2050. Assuming the best-case scenario of 40 billion m³, and that this brine waste is contained as a single spherical drop, the diameter would be just over 4 km, a diameter approximately the same as the length of the small principality of Monaco.

If, as seems likely, most of the new plants are in Asia, including the Middle East, and this utilises, in the main, RO-SW with brine production of 1.35 m³ per m³ of pure water, then the total brine waste produced in 2050 is higher at about 130 and 45 billion m³ for the *Heroic* and *Progressive* scenarios respectively.

Summary key points

- Scenario analysis is used to explore possible futures by considering how economic, social, and technical developments might evolve. Scenarios weave together the complex interactions between these developments, underpinned by detailed model projections.
- Several scenario exercises have been carried out that focus on, for example, energy and the related carbon dioxide emissions to the climate change milestone date of 2050 and on the implications for water resources.
- Overall domestic water demand is projected to grow significantly in the next three decades, doubling in the period to 2050. Asia, with its large population and continued rapid economic development, will consume almost 60% of the world total.
- Pure water produced by desalination is an increasingly important additional supply to water resources. The volume will continue to grow from its current level of about 95 million m³ per day to between 190 and 360 million m³ per day in 2050, and its contribution to the global domestic sector will likely lie between 7% and 14% of the total.
- RO will be the preferred technology, and an *indicative* number of between 7,000 and 20,000 additional new plants will be built in the next three decades; additionally, perhaps 8,000 larger plants will be needed to replace the existing fleet, in the period to 2050. The actual number of plants will depend on the scale of need of the communities involved. Asia, including the Middle East, will be particularly prominent in the deployment of new production capacity in this period.
- Energy will continue to be a key factor in the desalination industry, and electricity will be the main energy carrier in the future due to the dominance of RO. The industry will consume between 275 TWh and 520 TWh

in 2050, equivalent to the electricity consumed by a major developed country. Desalination may well emerge as the largest consumer of electricity in the water industry.

- The dominance of RO will have benefits for the environment. The move towards electricity lowers the carbon dioxide emissions per m^3 of pure water produced, and this will be improved further with the expected decarbonisation of the power sector. Overall, the carbon dioxide emissions from the industry will fall by at least a factor of two by the middle of the century.

- The environmental benefits associated with RO extend to the brine waste produced by the industry. Looking ahead to 2050, the daily desalination water production capacity could increase by a factor of between two and four; the brine waste associated with this pure water production will remain steady at about current levels for the former and increase by a factor of two at the higher water production rate.

7 Reflections

Desalination has emerged as a very important global industry, without which the provision of pure water would be very challenging in some regions.

7.1 Climate change to the fore

There are several drivers that have led to increased pressure on freshwater resources over the past 60 years, including population growth, economic development, migration from rural to urban centres, and climate change, with their relative importance in that order. In late 2022, the population reached the milestone of 8 billion people, which is about 2.5 times higher than it was in 1960, the date the desalination industry began to emerge in different parts of the world. Looking ahead, the UN using demographic data to extrapolate a historical trend suggests the global population would grow to about 9.7 billion people by the middle of this century and then continue rising to a peak of about 10.4 billion towards the end of the century.

More recently, a more holistic study commissioned by the Club of Rome incorporated social and economic factors and proposed two possible futures: a *'business-as-usual'* scenario and a more *'optimistic'* scenario. In the former, the global population peaks at 8.8 billion by about 2045 and then declines to 7.1 billion by 2100; in the optimistic scenario, the population peaks at 8.5 billion as early as 2040 and then falls to about 6 billion in 2100. This would be a remarkable outcome and reduce pressure on the natural environment, including freshwater water resources.

At worst, the population will *rise* by 25% over the next half century; at best, it will *rise* 10% by the middle of the century and then *decline* by 25% by the end of the century. These projections suggest that population growth is much less of a driver for freshwater resources in the future than it has been in the past.

Another aspect of population will continue to be important: the growth in urban population, in part due to migration from rural areas, particularly in developing countries. By 2050, projections suggest that almost 70% of the

DOI: 10.4324/9781003334224-7

world's population will live in urban areas, up from about 50% in the first decade of this century. As indicated in Chapter 2, this has major implications for energy, food, and water resources, both in terms of the increased scale of need and the infrastructure to deliver them.

Water demand and economic growth are intimately linked. The global economy has grown by up to about 6% per annum over the past 60 years, a trend only disturbed by financial crises, the latest in 2008, and the COVID pandemic in 2022, both of which resulted in negative growth at the global level. Economic growth going forward and the associated increase in living standards suggest that demand for freshwater will continue to rise. This demand can be alleviated by better management of the available freshwater resources, the adoption of innovative practices, and pricing that encourages a more sustainable use of water. However, despite such efforts, groundwater resources could continue to be depleted at unsustainable rates in some parts of the world.

The effects of climate change on water supplies are apparent today, and they will become even more so in the coming years and decades. Rising global temperatures and the associated drought conditions and longer term aridification will make many places uncomfortable for many months of the year; in extreme cases such places might become uninhabitable and encourage migration. There will also be increased frequency of extreme weather events such as wildfires, storms, and flooding, and these will cause disruptions, damaging infrastructure and disrupting water supplies.

All the indications are that climate change will place considerable pressure on the available freshwater resources, ahead of population growth and economic development, in the future. Desalination will be needed to maintain water supplies, primarily for domestic use but also, increasingly, to service the agriculture and industry sectors. In one sense, the industry is helping to *mitigate* the effects of increasing water scarcity due to climate change; in another sense, society is *adapting* to the new water-stressed environment by creating another source of pure water through technology.

Freshwater resources are precious. Table 7.1 summarises some of the key metrics for freshwater water and desalination in 2020 and 2050 projections; also included are the key issues of food production, energy, and environment associated with desalination industry operations. These metrics are put into context by comparison with aspects of the natural and built environment.

7.2 Desalination now a mature industry

The desalination industry has gradually emerged into the mainstream water market; it meets the needs for drinking water in water-scarce areas and, in some cases, is also used for irrigation purposes and industrial production. It is critically important in some countries and a very helpful contingency measure in others.

Table 7.1 Some key metrics related to desalination in context

Theme	Metric	Context
Freshwater resources	Surface freshwater availability is relatively stable and estimated at over 50,000 km³ per year	Combined volume of three largest freshwater lakes, Baikal in Southern Siberia, Tanganyika in Africa, and Superior in North America, is 54,100 km³[1]
	Estimated demand of 4,600 km³ per year in 2010 and between 5,500 and 6,100 km³ per year in 2050	Total freshwater volume contained in the three North American lakes of Huron, Ontario and Erie combined is 5,700 km³[2]
		A spherical drop with a diameter of about 22 km, or about the distance covered in a half marathon (just over 21km), contains 5,570 km³ of water
	Groundwater abstraction currently amounts to an estimated 800 km³ per year and will rise to 1,100 km³ per year in 2050	Equivalent to draining half the total freshwater in Lake Ontario in North America (1650 km³) every year[2]
		A spherical drop of water with a diameter of about 12 km, the height flown by a typical passenger airliner (almost 11km), contains 900 km³ of water
Desalination	Desalination production capacity: about 35 billion cubic meters, or km³, a year in 2020	About the volume of water that flows over the Victoria Falls in Zimbabwe each year[3]
		A spherical drop with a diameter of 4 km, or the length of the Principality of Monaco, contains 33.5 km³ of water
	Projected desalination production capacity of between 70 and 130 billion cubic meters, or km³, in 2050	The lower projected volume is the same as the estimated annual freshwater flowing over the Niagara Falls in Canada[3]
		A spherical drop with a diameter of about 6 km, or the height of Mount Logan in the Saint Elias Mountains in North America, contains 113 km³ of water[4]

(Continued)

Table 7.1 (Continued)

Theme	Metric	Context
Energy	An estimated 140 TWh was needed by the desalination industry in 2020	The total electricity of about 152 TWh consumed in Argentina, a country of almost 46 million, in 2021[5]
	A projected electricity consumption by the desalination industry of between 275 TWh and 520 TWh in 2050	The total electricity consumption of Spain and France in 2021 were 272 TWh and 547 TWh respectively[5]
Food production	Area of cultivated land: 1,540 million hectares in 2010 and between 1,620 and 1,775 million hectares in 2050	The land area of the Russian Federation is 1,640 million hectares[6]
	Land under irrigation: 320 million hectares in 2010 and between 355 and 375 million hectares in 2050	The combined area of Argentina and Chile is 348 million hectares[6]
Environment	Estimated total CO_2 emissions of about 214 million tonnes in 2020, declining to between 50 and 100 million tonnes in 2050	Emissions in 2020 are very similar to the emissions from energy use by Egypt, a country with a population of almost 110 million[5]
	Estimated volume of brine waste production of about 53 billion m³ in 2020	A spherical drop with a diameter of 4.7 km, or slightly longer than the length of the Principality of Monaco, contains over 54 km³ of water
	Indicative values for brine waste production of between 45 and 130 billion m³ in 2050	A spherical drop with a diameter of 6.3 km, or slightly higher than the height of Mount Logan in the Saint Elias Mountains in North America, contains 131 km³ of water[4]

Sources: (1), The Largest Lakes In The World By Volume, World Atlas, www.world-atlas.com; (2), Great Lakes water volume, US Environmental Protection Agency, www.epa.gov; (3), The World's Largest Waterfalls: By Average Volume, World Waterfall Database www.worldwaterfalldatabase.com; (4), The World's Tallest Mountain Ranges, The World Atlas, www.worldatlas.com; (5), BP Statistical Review, 2022; (6), Land area, World Bank Indicators, https://data.worldbank.org/, 2021.

Its evolution has followed the same path as has occurred in, for example, the renewables industry within the energy sector. A variety of desalination technologies were developed over time and used on a relatively small scale. The technical and engineering institutions came forward with innovations that not only improved existing technologies but also brought forward new concepts to address weaknesses, including those related to energy and the environment. A combination of innovation, increased scale, and supply chain maturity has led to more widespread deployment. Today, a significant number of technology designs exist, some in early development, some in pilot form, and yet others more advanced; there are at least three mainstream commercial technologies. The sector is rich in ideas and concepts, and combinations of technologies are not uncommon.

A vibrant supply chain has emerged, providing valuable secondary innovation and increased scale, largely to meet a growing demand for drinking water. This supply chain will continue to grow in the period to 2050 as major technological powers like China enter the international market to rival the more established companies from Europe, North America, and the Middle East.

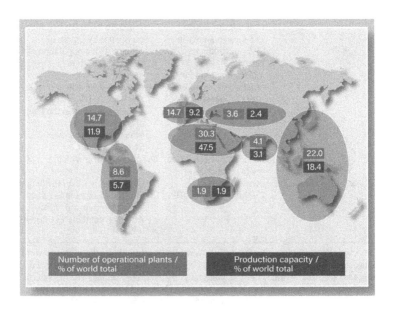

Figure 7.1 Regional distribution of plants and production capacity.

Source: The state of desalination and brine production, Edward Jones et al., Science of Total Environment, Volume 657, p1343, 2019.

Note: Reported total number of operational plants just under 16000; estimated total operational production capacity just over 95 million cubic metres a day.

Production costs have declined, in part due to increased scale, as traditionally occurs with learning, but also in the choice of technology. The latter is perhaps more influential in this industry because it involves, in part, a trade-off between energy consumption, a significant contributor to the overall cost of production, and water quality. The attributes of low energy consumption and water quality for domestic use are met by the 'winning' technology: Reverse Osmosis (RO). The latter is essentially a physical process that can be easily deployed and, once commissioned, can be operated and maintained by small teams. It can also be replicated relatively easily where it is needed and at a scale to match the level of water demand, the nature of feedwater resources available, or both.

This technology also benefits from using mechanical energy driven by electricity rather than thermal energy, and as such, is less carbon intensive; it will be even less so in the future as renewable electricity replaces fossil fuel generation. The brine waste produced is less saline than that from thermal technologies, in part due to the higher total dissolved solids retained in the pure water, but still well within that needed for domestic consumption.

Table 7.2 compares the past with the future for some of the key indicators that have implications for the desalination industry. It shows, for example, a new development phase for the industry in which climate change impacts increase, supply chain capability improves, and technology improvements and renewables integration decarbonise the energy used.

Table 7.2 Relative importance of key issues in relation to desalination

Themes	Key issues	Past[1]	Future[1]
Drivers for freshwater demand	Population growth	↑	→
	Migration rural to urban centres	↑	→
	Economic growth	↑	↑
	Climate Change impacts	→	↑
Freshwater Resources	Renewable resources at global level	→	→
	Groundwater resources depletion	↑	↑
Desalination industry	Pace of deployment	↑	→
	Part of mainstream water industry	→	↑
	Technology innovation	↑	→
	Supply chain development	↑	↑
Energy and Environment	Fossil fuel use	↑	↓
	Integration of renewable electricity	(2)	↑
	Carbon dioxide emissions	↑	↓
	Brine waste production	↑	→

Notes: (1), Author's assessment. The arrows indicate relative importance within each theme at the global level; the relative importance will differ by region and country; (2), little or no integration of renewables.

7.3   The outlook for desalination

Desalination has been deployed in most countries around the world, the scale dependent on local conditions and demand. The industry has demonstrated that it can meet water needs in very different environments, most pressing in the northern hemisphere between 0° and 40° latitudes but also in other parts of the world: in South America, Southern Africa, and Australia. Countries in Asia and Africa will have the largest populations going forward and will have the greatest need for this technology.

The most vulnerable in terms of water scarcity are islands and countries where low rainfall and aridification prevail or where the necessary infrastructure to allow the transport of water between regions has not been sufficiently developed. Crucially, it is difficult to see how society in those countries where renewable resources are not sufficient to meet water needs and groundwater supplies are being depleted could maintain economic and social well-being if desalination was not readily available. This is most striking in Saudi Arabia, where demand is well above renewable water resources and there is a heavy reliance on desalination. It is also difficult to see how this country, and others in the Middle East and North Africa with similar freshwater problems, can transition away entirely from using fossil fuels for desalination in the period to 2050.

The creation of natural reservoirs through river dams, improved infrastructure and more careful management of renewable and wastewater resources, and the gradual introduction of desalination have helped countries meet their water requirements thus far. Indeed, in arid countries such as Cyprus, there are practically no flowing rivers, such is the need for reservoirs to service the needs of its local population and the large influx of tourists every year. Here, the water authorities await the winter rains to help fill the reservoirs and then contract with the companies running the desalination plants to make up any projected shortfall.

Going forward, more desalination plants will be needed as weather patterns change and rainfall declines. It is fair to say that the industry has evolved from a national and regional actor to a global industry. The production capacity of the global fleet will continue to grow, with the scale dependent on the effects of climate change on renewable water resources. Water for the domestic sector will continue to increase across the world with rising populations, particularly in cities, and it is likely that the contribution of desalination will double in the period to 2050; in some countries, this contribution will likely be much higher.

The desalination production capacity, then, will increase significantly in the period to 2050, by at least a factor of two and perhaps as much as a factor of four. However, the average size of RO plant, is also expected to increase over this period, perhaps by a factor of two. The overall size of the global fleet will be determined by the number of new plants commissioned to deliver the increase in water production needed and replacement plants for those in the existing fleet that close over that period. In both cases, the global fleet of plants will likely have an average size greater than before, and they will be more efficient, but the local conditions will ultimately determine the size of plant deployed.

A major challenge will be to provide water in those regions where population growth is high, rural to urban migration continues at pace, or both. Further, internal renewable freshwater resources may be less available in some regions due to climate change, and the cost of production by desalination may be less affordable. Countries in northern and southern Africa are in this group.

Fossil fuel use in desalination will decline over the next three decades, primarily due to the move towards RO technology and the decarbonisation of the electricity sector already under way. The greatest change will be in those countries where the desalination capacity has grown significantly in the recent past and will continue to grow in the coming decades. It is also the case that there has been a heavy reliance on fossil fuels in these countries, either directly in thermal technologies or in the production of electricity. China, countries in the Middle East and North Africa, and North America must be at the forefront of the transition to low-carbon electricity, and the major deployment of renewables and nuclear power in these regions suggests this will be possible.

The use of thermal energy has been prominent in the desalination industry, but electricity has emerged as the key energy carrier for the industry going forward. The electricity needed to deliver the projected desalination water production by 2050 could rise by up to a factor of four. To put this into context, in absolute terms, electricity use by the sector was less than 0.5% of the total global consumption in 2021. The large projected increase in electricity consumed by 2050 will likely remain at this level, at least in percentage terms, since global electricity production will also rise significantly over this period. It is likely the existing facilities that utilise Multi-Stage Flash (MSF) and Multi-Effect Distillation (MED) technologies will be replaced with RO technology as they close at the end of their operational lives over the next two or three decades, and the considerable thermal energy used by the industry for these technologies will also decline.

As indicated above, the carbon intensity of the electricity used by the industry will decline going forward, and the amount of thermal energy will also decline as MSF and MED facilities are replaced. The total carbon dioxide emissions associated with the energy consumed, then, will also decline despite the large increase in production capacity of the fleet. These transitions will mean the carbon footprint of desalination will be less important in the future, so long as government agencies and industry deliver on its commitments under the Global Clean Water Desalination Alliance.

Brine waste production is also an important environmental issue. At best, and in absolute terms, this will remain at approximately the same level as it is today, about 50 billion m^3 in 2020, and at worst, the volume may increase by a factor of two in the period to 2050. When compared to the volume of water in a sea, the amount of brine waste discharged by the industry is very small, but it is nonetheless incumbent on the operators to ensure the efficient dilution of this effluent from their plants so that marine environments local to the sites are undamaged.

Overall, the desalination industry is in a very good position for its next stage of development in the crucial period to 2050. Challenges remain, particularly in reducing costs to a level which allows developing countries to deploy the technology and in dealing with environmental issues. Nonetheless, it has a good bedrock of knowledge, experience, and supply chain capability to help communities across the world meet their pure water needs.

Summary key points

- Pressure on water resources will continue to grow in the coming decades, with climate change, a key driver in increasing water scarcity.
- The deployment of desalination technology will continue at pace, with production capacity doubling and possibly quadrupling in the period to 2050, depending on the severity of the emerging water crisis.
- The cost of desalinated water can be high, but technological advances are expected to reduce costs by up to 60% over the next few decades.
- The supply chain capability for the desalination industry will be enhanced with new entrants into the market, and these will encourage further innovation and efficiency gains.
- The average capacity of the global desalination fleet will continue to rise with RO as the technology of choice. The existing fleet will be largely decommissioned by 2050, to be replaced by new, more efficient, and less polluting plants.
- Electricity consumption by the desalination industry will rise significantly in this period in sympathy with increasing global water production, primarily through RO, while thermal energy will decline as the main distillation plants close.
- Fossil fuel generation will give way to renewable and low carbon electricity, the pace and extent determined by the available resources and a drive to meet climate change targets; the relative costs and technical facility of candidate technologies will also play a role.
- The environmental impacts of desalination need not be an impediment to its growth. There will be some major changes in the two main waste streams: CO_2 and brine. Decarbonisation of the electricity sector will result in declining CO_2 emissions while the brine produced will rise, but at a lower rate than in the past.

Selected acronyms

Climate Change

NOAA	National Oceanic and Atmospheric Administration
CO_2	Carbon dioxide
CH_4	Methane
N_2O	Nitrous Oxide
SF_6	Sulphur Hexafluoride
AMOC	Atlantic Meridional Overturn Current
COP	Conference of the Parties
CRI	Climate Risk Index

Economic and societal

GDP	Gross Domestic Product
PPP	Purchasing Power Parity
HDI	Human Development Index
MENA	Middle East and North Africa
UAE	United Arab Emirates
USA	United States of America
UK	United Kingdom

Water resources

IWA	International Water Association
SDGs	Sustainable Development Goals
TDS	Total Dissolved Solids
GCWA	Global Clean Water Alliance
WPA	Water Purchase Agreement
SWPC	Saudi Water Partnership Company
IWP	Independent Water Plant
IWPP	Independent Water and Power Production
PPP	Public Private Partnership

Desalination

MED	Multi-Effect Distillation
MSF	Multi-Stage Flash Distillation
MVC	Mechanical Vapour Compression
TVC	Thermal Vapour Compression
RO	Reverse Osmosis
ED	Electrodialysis
RO-SW	Reverse Osmosis-Seawater
RO-BW	Reverse Osmosis-Brackish Water
MSF-SW	Multi-Stage Flash-Seawater
MSF-BW	Multi-Stage Flash-Brackish Water
MED-SW	Multi-Effect Distillation-Seawater
MED-BW	Multi-Effect Distillation-Brackish Water

Energy and environment

GCWDA	Global Clean Water Desalination Alliance
EIAs	Environmental Impact Assessments
kWh	Kilowatt-hour
MWh	Megawatt-hour
GWh	Gigawatt-hour
TWh	Terawatt-hour
PV	Photovoltaic
CSP	Concentrated Solar Power

Scenario analysis

UNEP	United Nations Environment Programme
IIASA	International Institute for Applied Systems Analysis
IEA	International Energy Agency
WEO	World Energy Outlook
NGO	Non-Government Organisations

Bibliography

The author has used information from many sources including institutional websites, papers published in learned journals, specialist presentations, and newspaper articles. Below are the main sources by chapter numbers; some references proved useful in several chapters but for simplicity and to avoid repetition are cited in the specific chapter in which these were first introduced as a source.

Chapter 1

Does Size Matter? Meet Ten of the World's largest Desalination Plants, Aquatech, 2021

Global land and ocean temperature anomalies 1880-2022, Erick Burgueño Salas, Statista, April 2023

Global Monitoring Laboratory, Earth System Research Laboratories, NOAA

Milestones from Desalination Plant History, Preceden, www.preceden.com

Ocean Circulation, Tipping Points, and the Public Climate Debate, Stefan Rahmstorf, EPA Climate Change Lecture, Dublin Mansion House, April 19th 2023

Statistical Review, BP, 2022

Valuing Water, The United Nations World Water Development Report, 2021

Who has contributed most to global CO_2 emissions? Hannah Ritchie, Our World in Data, 2019

World Development Indicators, World Bank, 2022

Water Use and Stress, Our World in Data, 2018

Chapter 2

2021 State of Climate Services: Water, World Meteorological Organisation, 2021.

Climate Change 2022: Mitigation of Climate Change, Working Group III contribution to the Sixth Assessment Report of the Intergovernmental Panel on Climate Change, United Nations, 2022

Groundwater. Making the Invisible Visible, The United Nations World Water Development Report, UNESCO, 2022

Global Climate Risk Index 2021, David Eckstein et al., Germanwatch Institute, 2021

Global Water Security, the Royal Academy of Engineering, 2011

How we feed the world today, OECD, www.oecd.org

Human Development Index, United Nations Development Programme, UNDP, 2022

Population Trends 1950-2100 Globally and within Europe, European Environment Agency, 2021

The Economist in Numbers, 2022

The Water Price Index, www.holidu.com, 2022

Urbanization, Hannah Ritchie and Max Roser, Published online at OurWorldInData. org., 2018

World Development Indicators, World Bank, 2022

Water Futures and Solutions, Peter Burek et al., IIASA, 2016

Chapter 3

A Review of Water Desalination Technologies, Domenico Curto et al., Applied Sciences, 11, 670, 2021

As water scarcity increases desalination plants are on the rise, Jim Robbins, Yale Environment 360, June 2019

Cities turn to desalination for water security, but at what cost? www.theconversation. com, February 11, 2019

Desalination of Seawater and Brackish water, Philippe Bandelier, www.Encyclopedie-Energie.Org, 2021

Desalination Post-Treatment Considerations, Steven J. Duranceau, Florida Water Resources Journal, November 2009

Does size matter? Meet ten of the world's largest desalination plants, Aquatrade.com, 2021

Energy-water-environment nexus underpinning future desalination sustainability. Mohammad W. Shahzad et al., Desalination, 413, 52–62, 2017

Integration of wind energy and desalination systems: A Review study, Fransesca Greco et al., ResearchGate, 2021

Investigation of carbon footprints of three desalination technologies: Reverse Osmosis (RO), Multi-Stage Flash Distillation (MSF) and Multi-Effect Distillation (MED), Huyen Trang Do Thi and Andras Josef Toth, Periodica Polytechnica Chemical Engineering, 2023

Multidimensional analysis of nexus technologies I: diffusion, scaling and cost trends of desalination, Beatriz Mayor, IIASA, 2018

Private Communication, Olivier Carret, 2021

Spanish desalination know-how, a world-wide benchmark, Laura F. Zarza, Smart Water Magazine, Feb 2022

The state of desalination and brine production, Edward Jones et al., Science of the Total Environment, 657, 1343–1356, 2019

Chapter 4

Electricity consumption in the water sector by process, 2014–2040, www.iea.org/articles/introduction-to-the-water-energy-nexus

Energy Consumption and Desalination, Juan Miguel Pinto, Energy Recovery Inc., 2020

Energy-water-environment nexus underpinning future desalination sustainability, Mohammad W. Shahzad et al., Desalination, 413, 52–62, 2017

Environmental impacts of desalination and brine treatment – Challenges and mitigation measures, Argyris Panagopoulos and Katherine-Joanne Haralambous, Marine Pollution Bulletin, 161, 2020

Global Clean Water Desalination Alliance, Climate Initiative Platform, UNEP, 2016

Investigation of carbon footprints of three desalination technologies: Reverse Osmosis (RO), Multi-Stage Flash Distillation (MSF), and Multi-Effect Distillation (MED), Huyen Triang Do Thi and Andras Jozsef Toth Periodical Polytechnic Chemical Engineering, 2023

Integration of Wind Energy and Desalination Systems: A Review Study, Francesca Greco et al., ResearchGate, December 2021

Linear Fresnel Concentrator with dual energy solar tracking Application: Seawater desalination, Mohamed Oulhazzan et al., European Journal of Scientific Research, 142, 72–80, 2016

Saudi Arabia's desalination plant water production 2010-2019, Salma Saleh, Statista, 2023

Saudi Arabia: Total population from 2017 to 2027, Statista, 2022

State-of-the-art of renewable sources used in water desalination: Present and future prospects, Jochem Bundschuh et al., Desalination, 508, 2021

Chapter 5

Climate Trends in Western Australia, Department of Primary Industries and Regional Development based on data from Water Corporation of Western Australia, 2020

Current situation and Challenges of desalination in Chile, Sebastian Herrera-Leon, Desalination and Water Treatment, 171, 93, 2019

Cyprus spent €460 million on desalinated water over the past six years, A. Nicolaou, https://in-cyprus.philenews.com., 19 June 2023

Cyprus Water Development Department, www.moa.gov.cy

Desalination in Morocco: status and prospects, Soufian El-Ghzizela et al., Desalination and Water Treatment, 1–15, 231, 2021

Ministry of Finance, Israel 2020 and 2021

Progress and Perspectives of Desalination in China, Guoling Ruan et al., Membranes, 11, 206, 2021

Spanish desalination know-how, a world-wide benchmark, Laura F. Zraza, Smart Water Magazine, 2022

Water in Saudi Arabia: Desalination, Wastewater, and Privatization, US-Saudi Business Council, 2021

Water in Spain: the challenge of dry land, we are water, 2022

Updated and Extended Survey of U.S. Municipal Desalination Plant, U.S. Department of the Interior Bureau of Reclamation, 2018

The role of desalination in Australia's changing climate, Utility Magazine, 2022

Chapter 6

CO_2 intensity of electricity generation worldwide from 2000 to 2050, by region, Ian Tiseo, Statista, 2023

Desalination - Past Present and Future, IWA, August 2016
Energy and Climate Change: World Energy Outlook Special Report, International Energy Agency, 2015
Water Energy Nexus, International Energy Agency, 2016
Water Futures and Solutions, Peter Burek, IIASA, 2016
World Water Development Report 2018: Nature-Based Solutions for Water, UNESCO, 2018

Chapter 7

BP Statistical Review, 2022
Great Lakes water volume, US Environmental Protection Agency, https://www.epa.gov
Land area, World Bank Indicators, https://data.worldbank.org/, 2021
Our growing population, www.un.org/en/global-issues/population, 2022
People and Planet: 21st century sustainable population scenarios and possible living standards within planetary boundaries. B. Callegari and P.E. Stoknes, Earth4All, March 2023, version 1.0
The Largest Lakes in the World by Volume, The World Atlas, www.worldatlas.com
The World's Largest Waterfalls: By Average Volume, World Waterfall Database www.worldwaterfalldatabase.com
The World's Tallest Mountain Ranges, The World Atlas, www.worldatlas.com

Index

Printed in the USA
CPSIA information can be obtained
at www.ICGtesting.com
LVHW010221180224
772060LV00002B/372